WORLD WAR II
WITNESS ACCOUNTS

WORLD WAR II WITNESS ACCOUNTS

BY JANICE ANDERSON

Abbeydale Press

This edition is published by Abbeydale Press, an imprint of Anness Publishing Ltd,
Hermes House, 88–89 Blackfriars Road, London SE1 8HA;
tel. 020 7401 2077; fax 020 7633 9499

www.annesspublishing.com

Anness Publishing has a new picture agency outlet for images for publishing, promotions or advertising.
Please visit our website www.practicalpictures.com for more information.

Produced by Omnipress Limited, UK
Cover design by Omnipress Limited, UK

ETHICAL TRADING POLICY

Because of our ongoing ecological investment programme, you, as our customer, can have the pleasure and
reassurance of knowing that a tree is being cultivated on your behalf to naturally replace the materials used to
make the book you are holding. For further information about this scheme, go to
www.annesspublishing.com/trees

JANICE ANDERSON was born and educated in New Zealand, but has lived for many years in
Britain. After working for some years as a newspaper journalist, charity press officer and editor for
several of Britain's leading illustrated non-fiction publishing companies, she became a freelance writer
and editor, specialising in illustrated non-fiction books. Like her late husband, Edmund Swinglehurst,
with whom she has written several books, Janice Anderson has written many non-fiction books,
specialising in art, cinema, travel and social history.

A CIP catalogue record for this book is available from the British Library.

Contents

Introduction   6

At War Again   11

The War on Land   29

The War in the Air   59

The War at Sea   85

War on the Home Front   109

The Beginning of the End   139

Victory   151

Introduction

World War II was the greatest conflict the world has ever seen, involving six years of death and destruction on a scale almost impossible to comprehend. It began just twenty years after the peace settlements that followed the Great War of 1914–1918 – the war that was supposed to end war.

The Treaty of Versailles, signed in 1919, was intended to clear the way for a peaceful future for Europe and the world. The defeated nation, Germany, accepted that it had been the guilty party and that it should pay reparations. The reparations set by the victorious Allies, led by President Woodrow Wilson of America, were so severe that Germany, humiliated and deprived of much of Europe considered to be German, quickly plunged into economic chaos.

Out of the chaos rose a man, Adolf Hitler, and a party, National Socialism (Nazi), determined to avenge the humiliations imposed on their country by the Treaty of Versailles and to wrest back those territories lost in 1919. Hitler became Chancellor of Germany in January 1933 and, on the death of President Hindenberg, Germany's outstanding Great War general, in August 1934, Head of State and Supreme Commander of Germany's armed forces.

Germany's increasingly threatening stance in Europe in the 1930s, the Civil War in Spain, in which Hitler put Germany's air power into action on the side of Franco (thus gaining invaluable experience of air combat), and Italy's invasion of Abyssinia, made the chances of continuing peace in

Europe look unlikely. Britain, looking on from what was seen as the comparative safety on other side of the English Channel, hoped that the country need not get involved in the problems of Europe and was slow to re-arm.

In August 1939 the movement towards war in Europe gathered pace. In Britain, there was even a trial 'blackout' in London on 9 August. Less than two weeks later, Britain's attempts to negotiate a non-aggression agreement with Russia broke down and on 23 August, Germany and Russia signed a Nazi-Soviet pact. A day later the British Parliament passed the Emergency Powers (Defence) Act, military reservists were called up and the ARP (Air Raid Precautions) services were told to stand by. Few were really surprised when war broke out again on 3 September 1939. Britain and France had treaty obligations with Poland and both declared war on Germany after Poland was invaded on 1 September.

Although the United States of America and Japan both declared their neutrality in 1939, there was enough bad feeling between these two countries on either side of the Pacific to make war between them, if not inevitable, then certainly on the cards. The bad feeling was largely provoked by Japan's imperial ambitions in China, with whom Japan had privileged trading status and between whom the undeclared war that existed for much of the 1930s turned into a formal declaration of war from Japan in July 1937. On the eve of the outbreak of war in Europe, the USA imposed a series of economic sanctions on China and Japan, which the Japanese government failed to make any headway in renegotiating.

The situation between the two had deteriorated badly by late 1941. In October, Japan got a new prime minister, the army general H'deki Tojo. In November, the USA, noting the effect of Japanese activities on British and Dutch trading interests in the Far East, sent an ultimatum to Japan demanding its withdrawal from China, and saying that if it did not, then Japan would suffer a total trade embargo on oil (from the Dutch East Indies) and steel.

Japan's reply was made on 7 December 1941, when it attacked the USA's Pacific Fleet at anchor in Pearl Harbor, Hawaii. It followed up this devastating attack with attacks on Britain's imperial possessions in Malaya and Hong Kong, and on Manila, Guam and Midway, all in the USA's sphere of influence. On 8 December the USA and Britain declared war on Japan. On 11 December Italy and Germany both declared war on the USA, which responded in kind. World War II was now a truly world-wide affair.

By the late autumn of 1942, Hitler's war gains stretched from the Atlantic to the Middle East and to Leningrad and the Arctic seas in the north-east, while Japan was threatening India from Burma and Australia from New Guinea. The Allies, although reeling, did not allow the Axis powers to have everything their own way. The possession of radar, a British invention, played a big part in helping the RAF win the Battle of Britain, and the breaking of Germany's Enigma code by a collection of academics and boffins hidden in Nissen huts in the Buckinghamshire countryside played an even bigger part in neutralising Germany's part in the war in the Atlantic.

If the first three years of the war were largely a story of German and Japanese successes, the last three became an epic tale of gradual fighting back and an increasing number of battles won and territories regained.

By mid-August 1945, World War II was over – officially, at least – and only at the enormous cost of dropping atomic bombs on Japanese cities. In reality, it would be weeks before the last Japanese forces surrendered – in Hong Kong on 16 September – and months, even years, before every serviceman and woman had returned to civilian life. It was years before rationing came to an end in Britain, and many more years before the damage to the infrastructures of entire nations were repaired and rebuilt. Many historians would say that the true end of World War II did not come until the Berlin Wall came down and the treaty that gave full independence to the reunited East and West Germanys was signed in Moscow in September 1990.

AT WAR AGAIN

At War Again

Almost up to the day that war was declared, there were still, according to a Mass Observation survey, many people in Britain hoping that it would not happen. Surely Britain, despite Germany's takeover of Austria in March 1938 and the invasion of Czechoslovakia on 1 October 1938 ('allowed for' in Chamberlain's Munich 'peace with honour' Agreement with Hitler), could come to some sort of arrangement that would avert war with Germany. It was right that Parliament should have decided in November 1938, after 'Kristallnacht', when many Jews were murdered, their shops looted and synagogues destroyed, and thousands of Jewish men were sent to concentration camps, to admit into Britain up to 10,000 Jewish children from Nazi Germany. But it was hoped that this would be as far into Europe as Britain would have to go – or as far into Britain as Germany would come.

The 'blitzkrieg' invasion of Poland, a country with which Britain had well-defined treaty obligations, on Friday, 1 September 1939 ended such hopes. The long-planned evacuation of children from the danger zones, mostly in southern England, began immediately, people began to search for the gas-masks that had been issued to everyone in the summer of 1938, the trenches that had also been started in that summer were now repaired and extended, notices went up directing people to the trenches and air-raid shelters, and sales of black-out materials, torches and batteries rocketed. Housewives began stocking up on essential foods.

The end to all hope came shortly after 11.15 a.m. on Sunday, 3 September. Many people could quote for years afterwards the words they heard on the wireless that morning. The Prime Minister, Neville Chamberlain, said:

'I am speaking to you from the Cabinet Room at 10 Downing Street. This morning, the British Ambassador in Berlin handed the German Government a final note, stating that unless the British Government heard from them by 11 o'clock that they were prepared at once to withdraw their troops from Poland, a state of war would exist between us. I have to tell you now that no such undertaking has been received, and that consequently this country is now at war with Germany.'

In great contrast to August 1914, when a cheering jingoism accompanied by violent anti-German behaviour had been the order of the day, Britain took the declaration of war in September 1939 quietly and stoically. The government's one anti-German action in early September 1939 was to bring in internment for those Germans and Austrians in Britain judged to be security risks.

Within hours of Chamberlain's speech, the Prime Minister of Australia, Robert Menzies, took his country to war on the side of Britain, as did, within days, the prime ministers of Canada, New Zealand and South Africa. Eire, Italy, Japan and the United States all declared their neutrality in the coming conflict.

Britain had done as little re-arming as possible during the early 1930s, hoping to avoid war at all costs, and was still far behind Germany's military production figures. Much planning had been done in the matter of civil defence, so that by September 1939 there were well-thought-out Air Raid Precautions (ARP) and Civil Defence systems in force, although the necessary ARP warden command posts, air-raid shelters, and ambulance services were by no means all ready for use. There were barrage balloons in the bright September skies, however, and plenty of sandbags ready to be piled round the entrances to buildings, underground stations and other strategic points.

The invasion of Poland had begun with an air attack on Polish airfields and communications centres. Many people expected similar attacks on Britain within minutes of Chamberlain's speech – an expectation not calmed by the immediate sounding of air-raid sirens in London and elsewhere – and rushed outside to check the skies for approaching enemy aircraft. The sirens were being tested, not used for real, but their sounding still induced fear and even panic in many. In fact, while the war at sea began in earnest almost immediately in the Atlantic, nothing much happened on land for months. Soon people began to talk of a 'phoney' war.

Many of the men swept into uniform in the weeks after war was declared found themselves facing the inconveniences of service life rather than its dangers and horrors. By Christmas 1939, the most important work for many servicemen was finding a Christmas tree to carry home on leave, or helping with the large Christmas post in post office sorting rooms. In fact, greater horrors than the war had created so far were discovered lurking in Britain's social services. The evacuation of children from the perceived danger zones involved both the breaking up of families on the one hand, and the discovery by respectable folk with jobs and houses, on the other, of the depths of deprivation that existed in Britain's inner cities.

The phoney war lasted until well into spring, 1940. The failure of a British campaign to mine the waters round neutral Norway, at the same time landing troops on Norway's coast in early April, was the beginning of its end. Germany invaded Norway just days after the British landed. The failure of the Norwegian campaign led to the resignation of Neville Chamberlain, who was replaced as Prime Minister by Winston Churchill on 10 May 1940, the day on which Germany invaded the Netherlands. In Western Europe, the real war had begun at last. Even then, some might have thought there was a faint chance of Britain keeping out of it. Hitler finally decided to invade Britain only after the British government rejected his peace overtures in June, launching Operation Sealion, intended to destroy the RAF, shortly after.

Muriel Tucker

Muriel, a Londoner, was 13 in September 1939. At 14, the outbreak of war having meant the postponement of the raising of the school leaving age to 15, she was old enough to leave school and start work.

I remember the bother with Czechoslovakia, and we thought there was going to be a war. My father certainly did – and we were quite prepared for it. Then of course it all blew over temporarily, and I remember Dad bought us a dolly each to celebrate, because it seemed as if it was going to be all right – and of course it wasn't.

> Dad bought us a dolly each to celebrate, because it seemed as if it was going to be all right . . .

From Imperial War Museum archive tape 5261, included in Forgotten Voices of the Second World War, Max Arthur; Ebury Press in association with the Imperial War Museum, 2005.

John Silbermann, then called Manfred

Came to England as a 13-year-old on one of the last Kindertransport trains to bring Jewish children to Britain from Germany in the summer of 1939.

After Kristallnacht, my parents knew we had to get out. Before, the attitude was that Hitler couldn't last forever, that the good old days would come back, fair play would return.

I said goodbye to my parents [at a Berlin railway station] with just a kiss and a wave. Of course they had no idea it would be the last time. The plan was that we would meet up again in the U.S. England was meant to be just a transit point… we were blindly convinced that it wouldn't take long to defeat the Germans. Six months and it would all be over.

[At Harwich dock] for me it was all very exciting. From our viewpoint Britain was a great country – it had an empire, it had a king, it had everything. In a field by the port we Jewish children of all ages played a game of football. It was free… no one was shouting at you. It was a different world.

… the attitude was that Hitler couldn't last forever …

From an article in The Times, 22 November 2008.

Former Bomber Command pilot, Sir Lewis Hodges

Remembers the first days and dark, unlit nights of the war.

In that August of 1939 I was on leave with my family in Wales, and I received a telegram from the squadron instructing me to report back to the station forthwith because it looked as if war was imminent. I remember entering the living quarters there and everything had been transformed. All the electric light bulbs has been removed and blue light bulbs had been installed, which gave it a ghostly atmosphere. No blackout had been installed in those early days.

At the outbreak of war on September 3rd 1939 I was in the hangars at Finningley with other members of the squadron listening to the broadcast by Neville Chamberlain that a state of war now existed between our country and the Germans. I remember this dramatic moment very clearly. We rushed out of the hangars on to the tarmac and looked towards the east coast expecting to see German bombers coming over immediately....

We were fully occupied because we had just received new equipment. Hampden bombers had arrived and we were geared up to a big training programme, particularly night flying. The first time I flew a Hampden at night it was a great shock, because on take-off one was used to seeing the lights of Doncaster in the distance. But on this occasion it was pitch dark, no horizon, not a light to be seen.

From Bomber Command 1939-45, Richard Overy; HarperCollins Publishers, 1997.

Neville Chamberlain's wireless address to the nation

On 3 September 1939 Chamberlain's wireless address became an important memory for many children, including this boy called Kevin, who lived near Cardiff.

I remember my brother and I and our parents gathering round our small Bakelite wireless, bought specially because of the crisis – the first one we had.

From Children of War, Susan Goodman; John Murray, 2005.

Pam Ashford

Pam Ashford, a secretary in a coal shipping firm in Glasgow, kept a diary for Mass Observation throughout the war.

Tuesday, 29 August [1939]

In the office a certain amount of 'merriment' prevails in regard to the first-aid equipment, gas masks, incendiary bombs, etc. (like the 'We shall all do the goosestep' attitude of 1914). People regard gas masks askance.

The public morale is immeasurably higher than at the black points in the September crisis last year. Mr Mitchell (my boss), who has been spending a holiday in Millport, returned today, which is a day earlier than he was due. He believes the war will last 10/20 years. Miss Carswell openly says 'she has the wind up'. Everybody else agrees that if we show Hitler we are afraid, he will press his point....

On the way home I bought an electric torch and battery, and looked at stuff for ARP [Air Raid Precautions] curtains for the dining room. It would cost at least £1 to darken. I think I will wait to see what happens.

Thursday, 31 August

The department in which I work (exporting) is, of course, the one that ultimately will be most hit. Many of the trawlers that we normally bunker are at Grangemouth being fitted as minesweepers.

Afternoon: hope of a solution is rapidly declining, and tension rises every minute. Glasgow schoolchildren are to be evacuated tomorrow.

After work I made a purchase of electric torches. Notice the gradation: on Monday I bought a 6d [sixpenny] torch and spare battery; on Wednesday a 1/6 [one shilling and six pence] torch and battery. On Thursday two 1/9 torches plus one battery and two spare globes. Yesterday Mother got a spare battery for her torch.

I then went along to Massey's and bought three tins of new potatoes and 2lb of sugar. I also bought at Craig's four 6d jars of butter substitutes (grapefruit butter, lemon curd, apricot curd, banana curd).

Friday, 1 September
In the afternoon we heard that six children ranging from six to eleven had arrived at our Managing Director's house in Carluke. They are from Tradeston, a working class district with much slum property. Mr Ferguson, who likes children and is believed to wish he had several of his own, is delighted about it. He has bought camp beds and blankets and says that to fit the children up has cost him pounds.

Everybody agrees that if we show Hitler we are afraid, he will press his point . . .

From We Are At War, Simon Garfield; Ebury Press, 2005.

Doris Scott

Was a young mother living in Canning Town, London, in September 1939.

I was terrified of what would happen, since I had been through the First World War.… The air power of the First World War wasn't anything like that of 1939, but those raids were frightening enough.…

We were told that we all had to go to the local town hall and receive gas masks. My baby had to be issued with a sort of diving helmet with horizontal wires, totally encasing her. My other daughter was three, and had this Mickey Mouse gas mask which wouldn't scare her. My mother, being asthmatic, was given another contraption, which was right for her breathing – and I had the normal mask that everyone else did. So we had four different types of gas mask in one family.

> My other daughter was three, and had this Mickey Mouse gas mask which wouldn't scare her.

From Imperial War Museum archive tape 6383, included in Forgotten Voices of the Second World War, Max Arthur; Ebury Press in association with the Imperial War Museum, 2005.

Kenneth Morris

Recalls the early months of the war, in which his home life changed dramatically, but nothing much of a warlike nature happened.

When the news of the German invasion of Poland on 1 September came through on the wireless... my family knew that British guarantees to Poland meant that war was near. In the obscurity of the west London suburb of East Sheen, we shaded our lights and blacked out our windows in case a German blitzkrieg [lightning strike] came our way.

Like millions of others, I listened on Sunday 3 September to Neville Chamberlain's measured tones announcing that from 11 am a state of war existed between Britain and Germany. I was 18. I waited with some excitement for dramatic developments in the west; but waited in vain.

Daily life did not continue unchanged. On 1 September my brother Malcolm had been evacuated with the City of London School to Marlborough. Three days later my widowed father, who had served as an artillery officer in the first world war, was dispersed with his finance firm from central London to a manor house on the Derbyshire-Staffordshire borders. There he later happily assumed the roles of village squire and major commanding the Home Guard.

Document file Morris, K. W., 87/44/1 in the Documents Department of the Imperial War Museum.

Eileen Potter

A London County Council social worker and evacuation officer of West London, kept a diary for Mass Observation for the first year of the war.

Friday, 1 September

Arrive at East Acton Station at 7.15. I am put on telephone duty. The station is a small one, with a narrow, wooden platform reached by a flight of wooden stairs. At first, ordinary passengers arrive for the trains, but the station is theoretically closed to the public at about 8 o'clock. The first evacuation train is timed for 8.15. The children from the nearest school arrive considerably before then. They march up in good order, accompanied by teachers and helpers and all carrying kit and gas masks. The elder children of a family help the younger ones along. Some of the mothers and fathers come to see them off, but have to say goodbye at the station entrance as there is no spare room on the small platform. All are cheerful looking – hardly any tears – but I feel rather a lump in my throat at seeing them all going off so cheerfully.

> The elder children .. . help the youger ones along.

From We Are At War, Simon Garfield; Ebury Press, 2005.

Christopher Tomlin

Class-based reactions to evacuees, such as those noted by Lancashire writing paper salesman Christopher Tomlin, were common throughout Britain.

Friday, 1 September

The first thing I remember is the arrival of evacuees at Broughton. Four girls left a motor-car, and what 'things' they were! Dressed in 'old clo' man coats, dirty, common, the last kiddies in the world for an 'aristocratic' spot like Broughton.

In spite of the shock the evacuees gave me, I'm afraid a lump rose in my throat when one girl asked nervously, 'Can't I stay with my sister?' She was told, 'No, you go there, and she will be across the road. You will be able to see her every day.' I was sorry for the girls because they were so forlorn.

Monday, 4 September

There was much talk about evacuees. I heard that the children were filthy, bug-ridden, wore dirty clothes, would not eat proper food for they wanted toast and fish and chips. Some of the kids had to wear fresh clothes. Many housewives brought their guests a complete rig-out from pyjamas to coats.

There was much talk about evacuees.

From We Are At War, Simon Garfield; Ebury Press, 2005.

Fitzroy Maclean

The military career of Fitzroy Maclean, recently resigned from the Diplomatic Service, begins inauspiciously in 1939.

After swearing the Oath and filling in a number of forms, I was given the King's Shilling and a railway warrant to Inverness. I was a Private in the Cameron Highlanders, my father's old regiment.

I arrived at Inverness with a batch of several hundred other new recruits, for the most part nineteen-year-old youths from Glasgow. It was cold and grey and drizzling. In moist, undecided groups, we hung about the barrack square, our hands in the pockets of our civilian suits.

Then, suddenly, we were pounced on by half a dozen N.C.O.s. And given numbers. And divided into squads. And herded into bleak-looking barrack-rooms named after battles in the Peninsular War: Salamanca, Corunna, and Cuidad Rodriguez. And issued with things: boot brushes, tooth brushes, knife, fork, spoon, blankets, boots, overalls (denim), bonnets (Balmoral). And told not to —ing lose them. And told to look out and look sharp and hurry up, and use our —ing initiative. And given mops and pails and scrubbing brushes and told to —ing scrub the —ing floor.

From Eastern Approaches, Fitzroy Maclean; Jonathan Cape, 1949.

Mike Austin-Smith

Guarding VPs (Vulnerable Points) in London became one of the first duties of architecture student Mike Austin-Smith when, having volunteered as an other rank in the Artillery Regiment of the Honourable Artillery Company in April 1939, he was embodied into the Regular Army as an Other Rank on 31 August 1939.

23 October 1939

Dear Mother and Father

I am sorry I haven't written to you before this, but we have been very busy just recently as we have been getting ready to come down here and guard Battersea Bridge. We all look very efficient with tin hats, rifles and bayonets and great coats. We arrived here on Saturday morning and took over guard straight away but were relieved at four in the afternoon and had 24 hours off duty which consisted of nothing but fatigues . . .

I am sitting outside the guard room on the North Side of the Bridge, which is situated in the Yard of an Asphalt works, and surrounded by the Fulham Gas Light and Coke Company's works and Chelsea Power Station, so the surroundings and atmosphere are not exactly first class. The South guard room is a hut on an old derelict Greyhound track . . .

The guard that was here before us talked a lot about the I.R.A. throwing bricks on the bridge by means of a catapult . . .

From Life, Love and War: Letters Home 1939-1946, *by Mike Austin-Smith; privately printed – with kind permission of his widow.*

Evelyn Waugh, author

Evelyn Waugh's description of his first days in the army, in a letter to his wife, Laura, dated 10 December 1939, suggests that, so far, the war is indeed a 'phoney war', having introduced nothing more than a few inconveniences into life in the officers' mess.

So far, I have enjoyed myself very much. In the train at Victoria I recognized one of the men who had been in the medical exam. at the same time as I.… He was younger than me but looked older on account of having lost his wool. He was the type I expected to find – a Plymouth solicitor… who spent all his spare time sailing round Iceland. The rest of our draft, however, are a great surprise. There are 12 of us chosen out of our 2,000 applicants, no one least of all ourselves can conceive how. It is the main topic of speculation.… In fact [we are] the kind of nondescript body one might have conscripted out of the first omnibus one saw in the Strand.…

The regular Marines are very pleasant, hospitable people obsessed by their own obscurity. So far from the critical reception I expected…, the atmosphere has been one of ceaseless apology & self-deprecation in the Chinese style of courtesy 'Will noble and honourable second lieutenants deign to enter our unworthy mess and meet our ill-favoured Brigade Major?' As soon as we arrived we were surrounded by jaggering colonels & majors who stood us drinks continually from 12 noon until 11 p.m.

From The Letters of Evelyn Waugh, edited by Mark Amory; Weidenfeld & Nicolson, 1990.

THE WAR ON LAND

The War on Land

World War II's war on land effectively began on 10 May 1940, when German forces invaded the Netherlands and began a blitzkrieg sweep through the Ardennes into Belgium. Their aim was to split the French forces massed with the British Expeditionary Force (BEF) at the Channel coast side of northern France from the French forces dug in along France's 'impregnable' Maginot Line further east. The German blitzkrieg was so successful that within two weeks the BEF and the French were trapped in a pocket of country between Lille and the coast at Dunkirk.

Although Winston Churchill was able to turn the rescue of 220,000 British troops and 120,000 French troops from the beaches of Dunkirk into a morale-booster for the nation, it was a major defeat, easing Hitler's invasion of France, where French resistance collapsed on 5 June, and inspiring Mussolini's Italy to declare war on Britain and France on 10 June.

Italy's entry into the war ensured that North Africa, where Italian forces were concentrated in Libya and where British-occupied Egypt was a vital section of the route to India, was now in the forefront of the war on land. Soon, it also meant that the Balkans and Greece would be drawn into the conflict, Mussolini's ambitions leading him to invade Greece in November 1940.

In neither North Africa, where the

British began a campaign against the Italians which resulted in the capture of Tobruk in January 1941 and the surrender of the Italian forces at Beda Fomm in February, nor Greece, where the Greeks defeated the Italians and managed to drive them back into Albania in November 1940, did Italy turn out to be a strong Axis partner. Hitler took matters in Africa and in the Balkans into his own hands.

In early 1941 a small German armoured force, led by Lieutenant General Erwin Rommel, landed in Tripoli. Rommel's Afrika Korps, as it came to be called, defeated the British at Al Agheila in April, recovering all of Cyrenaica that the Italians had lost, except Tobruk, and taking many Allied prisoners-of-war in the process, by the end of the month. Meanwhile, another German army swept through Yugoslavia in April, driving the Allied forces out of Greece and on to the island of Crete, from where they retreated back to Egypt, leaving behind thousands of men to become prisoners-of-war.

While North Africa now became the major theatre of war for the Allies' land forces, Germany, in the ascendant, opened another front in eastern Europe. Operation Barbarossa was the name Hitler gave to his invasion of the USSR which began on 22 June 1941 and ended on 5 December, with Germany fully committed, but facing an unexpectedly strong and determined Soviet counter-attack. In the opening weeks of Barbarossa the German army lost 100,000 men and by December 1941 they were bogged down in what was to become the epic 900-day siege of Leningrad.

In December 1941, following Japan's attack on Pearl Harbor, another front, far from Europe, had opened. Once into the war, Japan began attacking British, Australian and American interests throughout Southeast Asia and the Far East. One after the other, British imperial possessions from Hong Kong to Singapore to Burma, on the border with India, still the jewel in Britain's imperial crown, fell into Japanese hands. Thousands of Allied servicemen were imprisoned, often in conditions similar to those that prevailed in Germany's concentration camps, and were put to work on roads and railways to help the Japanese war effort. The war in Burma, far from Europe and given little coverage in newspapers or on the radio, became one of the 'forgotten wars' of World War II.

Although men of the US Army fought an extraordinarily savage war against the Japanese in the Pacific, fighting in places as far apart as Bataan and Burma, Guadalcanal and the Philippines, the exploits of America's army in Europe grabbed much more attention. From January 1942, when American GIs began arriving in Britain, to be followed by massive amounts of arms and equipment, the war in Europe had an almost exclusive hold on the world's attention.

America joined the Allies in Africa in November 1942, when three-quarters of the 107,000-men-strong force landed on the beaches of Morocco and Algeria during Operation Torch were American. Operation Torch was led by the US forces commander, Dwight D. Eisenhower, who a year later would be named as Allied Supreme Commander for the invasion of north-west Europe.

Operation Torch took place four days after General Montgomery and the British Eighth Army won the decisive second Battle of El Alamein. Church bells were rung in England for this victory, but Winston Churchill was careful to say that 'this is not the end, it is not even the beginning of the end, but it is, perhaps, the end of the beginning.'

More great strides along the road towards the beginning of the end were soon being taken, both in eastern Europe, where the Soviet Union began a massive counter-attack against Germany at Stalingrad in November 1942, and in southern Europe, with the Allies landing in Sicily in July 1943 and making it to the Italian mainland in September. Already a D-Day for Normandy was being planned, and by the end of the year, men were being taken out of the Italian campaign and returned to Britain to prepare for it.

Signalman George Jones

His experience of the BEF's retreat to Dunkirk was typical of many.

Twice we took wrong turnings, almost walking down the throat of the enemy . . .

Pinned down, movement outside became impossible, but at least the same could be said for the enemy and since our ... cellar remained impervious to shot and shell we... [sat] back to rest, wait and hope for the best....

For us, our first miracle of Dunkirk... began... The curtain of ragged steel began to lift just before 10 p.m., and in the bright glow of a hundred fires, we walked from Furnes without a bomb, shell or bullet arriving within half a mile of our scrambling single files. Twice we took wrong turnings, almost walking down the throat of the enemy, but stumbling over piles of rubble, bricks, broken glass and tangled telephone wires, at last we were

From Wilson, Dunkirk: From Disaster to Deliverance, *quoted in* Dunkirk: Fight to the Last Man, *Hugh Sebag-Montefiore; Penguin Books, 2007.*

Fitzroy Maclean

A young diplomat before the war, Fitzroy Maclean discovered that joining the SAS did not guarantee a warm and pleasant Cook's tour in Eygpt in 1941.

Special Air Service Headquarters were in the Suez Canal Zone. I travelled down [from Cairo] with two Sergeants coming back from leave in a truck that was full of tommy-guns and parachutes and packets of high explosive. It was a long bleak drive. A bitter wind filled one's eyes with sand and chilled one to the bone. On either side of the narrow tarmac road, with its never-ending stream of cars and trucks, the desert stretched away dismally. From time to time we passed camps and dumps: huts and tents and barbed wire and signposts and clouds of flies, an uninviting smell of food rising from the cookhouses; the sickly smell of disinfectant rising from the latrines.

> . . . with its never-ending stream of cars and trucks, the desert stretched away dismally.

From Eastern Approaches, *Fitzroy Maclean; Jonathan Cape, 1949.*

Evelyn Waugh, author

The author writes to his wife Laura from Egypt, after serving as Robert Laycock's intelligence officer during the retreat from Crete. Waugh felt that abandoning Crete, leaving behind 12,000 men to become POWs, was a military disgrace.

I sent you a birthday present of cigarettes by Peter Fleming. I should have liked to send eggs, and chocolate and quails and silk stockings and all the things you must need but he could carry so little I thought Lucky Strikes the most acceptable thing…

Since I wrote last to you I have been in a serious battle and have decided I abominate military life. It was tedious and futile and fatiguing. I found I was not at all frightened; only very bored & very weary. For the time being I am delivered from countless perils to life and liberty. I shall have a great deal more to tell you when we meet which I cannot write now. Meanwhile, be profoundly grateful to God and his saints for my preservation during the days May 28 – June 1 [1941].

> Since I last wrote to you I have been in a serious battle …

From The Letters of Evelyn Waugh, *edited by Mark Amory; Weidenfeld & Nicolson, 1990.*

Fitzroy Maclean

With an SAS operation against the enemy-held port of Benghazi in Libya.

. . . hot bully stew, tea and sometimes a tot of rum.

After driving for twelve hours or more, the evening halt would be something to look forward to. Night falls quickly in the desert and the air grows suddenly cold. All at once you would feel the need of every scrap of clothing you possessed. Supper did not take long to prepare: hot bully stew, tea and sometimes a tot of rum. It was cooked over a desert fire, made by pouring some petrol into a tin filled with sand, which then burned with a steady flame for a surprisingly long time. After we had eaten, and filled our water-bottles from the water-tank in preparation for the following day, we would sit round the fire muffled in our greatcoats. Sometimes when the days signals had been sent, the wireless would be turned on to more frivolous uses and we would listen to jazz music, or to Tommy Handley, or to the eight o'clock news from London. Or to Lili Marlene, the new German chanteuse, singing her special song for the Afrika Corps from Radio Belgrade, now in enemy hands. [Lili Marlene was the name of the song.]

> *Unter der Lanterne,*
> *Vor dem grossen Tor…*

From Eastern Approaches, *Fitzroy Maclean; Jonathan Cape, 1949.*

Subaltern Ian Bell

Ian Bell was both impressed and repelled by General Erwin Rommel when he encountered him in the Western Desert in May 1942.

I could not stand any more of this and decided, in an angry mood, to go down to Rommel's headquarters. As I was talking to an interpreter, General Rommel himself came in....

So this master of cunning and genius of modern warfare was actually facing me now. He bore no distinct emblems of a German general and was wearing a soft peaked cap, faded by long service in the desert. Shorter than I, but stouter, he looked like the man I had always pictured him to be – strong and powerful, both physically and mentally.

The appetite for power was written across his ruddy countenance, with its covering of fine desert sand. His clothes were much worn and filmed with sand. His boots no longer shone with a high polish. Yet the man himself left a lasting impression on one's mind. I took the opportunity of looking him straight in the face and observed the cruel determination in his eyes....

Addressing the interpreter, he enquired what I was doing in the tent. Satisfied with the reply, General Rommel spoke to me in halting English, saying how sorry he was about the situation [of the prisoner-of-war camp, set right in the line of Allied fire] and that he would personally come to have a look at our fellows. Then, with a confident air as though assured his next

He bore no distinct emblems of a German general and was wearing a soft peaked cap, faded by long service in the desert.

moves against us would be successful, he calmly turned and went into his private tent. Thus ended my interview with the famous German general.

His cocksure bearing and complete disregard of danger compelled me to admire him. Whatever else he was, at least he was a good soldier.

Later that afternoon Rommel drove up to keep his word. He looked at the men from his lofty perch in his staff car with complete and callous unconcern....He turned to me and curtly said that transport would arrive some time that evening to evacuate us as a gap had been forced through to Timini. Then his car sped away back to his tent, causing more aggravating dust to float in our direction.

Report file Bell, R. I., 87/34/1 in the Documents Department of the Imperial War Museum.

Kenneth Morris

Served as an 'ordinary soldier' with HQ Squadron, 4th Armoured Brigade, in the Western Desert in 1942 and 1943.

Bare though the desert was, it was home for many pests, scorpions and millipedes, scorpion spiders and lizards, and even snakes. There were revolting flying beetles, blindly attracted by smells of putrefaction. Sand ticks, too, were troublesome, hard unsquashable little insects which tried to burrow under the skin to lay their eggs. Once I had to visit the M.O. as a sand tick had clamped onto my navel and would not be dislodged. Finally the M. O. removed it bodily with a pair of forceps, remarking that he never expected to use them in the desert.

But the greatest scourge of the desert was flies. Some were little more than midges. Most were house flies in size, though far more persistent. They settled on mess-tins of food, on mugs of tea, on spoons moving to our mouths, and on our mouths. They would buzz round our heads indefatigably, then dive suicidally into a mug of tea. Even more unpleasant were the huge sand flies, larger than bluebottles, which settled indiscriminately on excreta and food. All were potential carriers of disease, and most of the squadron suffered at some time from dysentery and desert sores, often slow to heal.

Report document Morris, K. W., 87/44/1 in the Documents Department of the Imperial War Museum.

Wallace Reyburn, Canadian war correspondent

Describes how Lieutenant–Colonel C.C.I. Merritt won the Victoria Cross during the disastrous Dieppe Raid in August 1942, from which only half of the 5,000 Canadians, 1,000 British, 50 American Rangers and handful of Free French who took part returned to England.

As the men [of the South Saskatchewan Regiment] got ready to tackle the bridge [over the River Scie in Dieppe] again, an officer came walking up the street. It was Colonel Merritt. He stopped and spoke to us, taking his tin hat off and mopping the perspiration off his brow as he did so. 'What's the trouble?' he asked. 'That bridge is a hot spot, sir. We are trying to get across it.' 'Okay, come with me.' Merritt walked out into the middle of the street again and said, 'Now men, we're going to get across this bridge. Follow me. Don't bunch up. Spread out. Here we go!' And he strode off to the bridge, erect, calm and determined-looking. He showed no sign of concern at the muck that was flying around him. His tin hat dangled from his wrist and he twirled it round as he walked. Most of the men got across this time. Merritt, himself, before that day was through, was to cross that bridge no fewer than six times....He was on the beach as the last of his men left in the subsequent withdrawal, but then, taking some spare Tommy guns and rifles, went back towards Pourville saying, 'I'm going to get even with these swine for what they have done to my regiment.'

From The Normandy Battles, *Bob Carruthers & Simon Trew; Cassell & Co., 2000.*

Sergeant John Longstaff

Was serving with the 2nd Battalion, Rifle Brigade, in the Western Desert when General Montgomery paid them a visit.

Montgomery came to the southern sector of the Alamein front at Alam Halfa, and one of the first things he asked was, when did we leave England and had we had any post? Not a single soldier had had a letter. Had we had any NAAFI [Navy, Army and Air Force Institutes, which provided mobile shops and canteen]? We hadn't even seen the NAAFI. We were scrounging as much as we could from other units – cigarettes – and understandably, other units weren't prepared to give them away or even sell them. He wanted to know why our shirts were stained – because we only had one shirt, and there was sweat – and they were hard, like bloody cardboard. He wanted to know if we'd had any leave. Nobody had had any leave at that stage. He made sure his adjutants took note of everything. He wasn't talking to the officers – he was talking to the riflemen – he was sitting inside little dugouts with the lads.

Before Montgomery, we never knew what our role was – where we were going, what was going to happen, who was on our left flank, right flank – who were our reserves. We didn't even know who the enemy was prior to Montgomery.... When a man is told these things, he starts getting confidence. He doesn't feel that he's fighting by himself.

From Forgotten Voices of the Second World War, *Max Arthur; Ebury Press, 2005 (p/b ed.).*

Unknown German soldier

The German soldier who wrote this first-hand account of the Battle of Stalingrad, if still alive when Field Marshal Paulus surrendered to the Soviet Sixty-Fourth Army on 31 January 1943, would have been lucky to survive the Russian POW camps: only 5,000 of the 108,000 Germans taken prisoner after the Battle of Stalingrad returned home.

. . . the sour smell of hopelessness.

It is hard, often impossible to distinguish between night and day, for vast clouds of smoke blot out the light. We live a semi-troglodyte existence in ground which shudders without pause from shellfire and amid a noise which stuns the senses. The darkness is often broken by the flames of the rocket projectiles – the Katyushas, which the Ivans have learned to mass in whole regiments so as to saturate selected areas of the battlefield. The rocket flames have scarcely died before the missiles in hundreds and thousands crash around us. They aim at no specific target, nor can our gunners… distinguish between the Ivans and ourselves, for our positions are too intermingled to permit accuracy. Russian rockets kill Russian Army men. Our artillery buries us during our bombardments. Stalingrad stinks of the corrupting dead, of fire, of destruction, and the sour smell of hopelessness.

From The World At Arms: The Reader's Digest Illustrated History of World War II; *Reader's Digest Association, 1989.*

Martin Ranft

A gunner in the 220th Artillery Regiment of Rommel's Afrika Korps, was on the receiving end of the opening barrage of the first Battle of El Alamein in 1942.

El Alamein was my home for quite a while, because we were stopped. On the 23rd October, nine o'clock in the evening, that's when we heard that terrible artillery fire from the British line. I was facing the front line and suddenly the whole sky was red with gunfire. The shells were howling over you and exploding all around you – it was just horrible. We thought then that the world was coming to an end.

> I was facing the front line and suddenly the whole sky was red with gunfire.

From Forgotten Voices of the Second World War, *Max Arthur; Ebury Press, 2005 (p/b ed.).*

Captain David Smiley

What was 'terrible' for Martin Ranft was 'tremendous' for Captain David Smiley of the Royal Armoured Car Regiment at El Alamein.

I was pretty impressed the night of Alamein, when the guns opened up. It was tremendous. All our searchlights were facing upwards in the sky to make a false daylight, to make things easier. When we went through the minefields and got to the first positions, there were dead Italians everywhere.... The barrage had opened up so suddenly, it had caught them well and truly unprepared.

When we went through the minefields and got to the first positions, there were dead Italians everywhere . . .

From Forgotten Voices of the Second World War, *Max Arthur; Ebury Press, 2005 (p/b ed.).*

Captain Harry Butcher, General Eisenhower's naval aide

Sums up in his diary how Ike, in his country cottage 'somewhere in England', with only the BBC news bulletins to keep him informed, remained confident that Monty and the Eighth Army would defeat Rommel at El Alamein.

During the evening [25 October 1942] we listened to the radio news and found practically all of it much more encouraging thaN at any other time since we have been here. The El Alamein battle has been launched, with General Montgomery announcing initial successes. Ike says that if quality and quantity of matériel and men can count in desert warfare against the wily Rommel, then Montgomery should win. He has 300 new Sherman tanks with 75s in completely revolving turrets. The obnoxious German 88s, which raised havoc with the British at Tobruk and through the retreat to El Alamein, will be countered by mobile 105s. Everything is being put into this operation, and it should succeed. Desert warfare, however, is difficult – as if any warfare were easy. Under the light cover of sand there is limestone, in which slit trenches are cut. It takes almost a direct hit to knock out such a trench. The British are laying a heavy barrage just as in World War I, with infantry to follow to neutralize mine fields and especially to cut through a path over which tanks and artillery may follow. With air superiority for the Allies, the equipment, men, and the will to win, we should turn the tide at last.

... Montgomery should win. He has 300 new Sherman tanks with 75s in completely revolving turrets.

From Three Years with Eisenhower, *Captain Harry C. Butcher, USNR; William Heinemann, 1946. Originally published in New York by Simon and Schuster.*

Fitzroy Maclean

Was parachuted into the Balkans in 1943 to make contact with the Partisans in Yugoslavia and their leader, Tito.

With a jerk my parachute opened and I found myself dangling, as it were at the end of a string, high above a silent mountain valley, greenish-grey and misty in the light of the moon.... Somewhere above me the aircraft, having completed its mission, was headed for home. The noise of its engines grew gradually fainter in the distance. A long way below me and some distance away I could see a number of fires burning. I hoped they were the right ones, for the Germans also lit fires at night at different points in the Balkans in the hope of diverting supplies and parachutists from their proper destinations. As I swung lower, I could hear a faint noise of shouting coming from the direction of the fires... Then... there was a jolt and I was lying in a field of wet grass....

The noise of its engines grew gradually fainter in the distance.

Then… there was a jolt
and I was lying in a field of wet grass….

Then, scrambling through a hedge, I came face to face with a young man in German uniform carrying a sub-machine gun. I hoped the German uniform was second-hand. *'Zdravo!'* I said hopefully. *Ja sam engleski oficir!'* At this the young man dropped the sub-machine gun and embraced me, shouting over his shoulder as he did so:

'Nasao sam generala! – I have found the general!' Other Partisans came running up to look at me. They were mostly very young, with high Slav cheek-bones and red stars stitched to their caps and wearing a strange assortment of civilian clothes and captured enemy uniform and equipment.

From Eastern Approaches, *Fitzroy Maclean; Jonathan Cape, 1949.*

Jack Swaab

A field gunner in the 51st Highland Division, records in his diary events in the last nervy, restless weeks of the 8th Army's time in North Africa.

9 May

Since I wrote, Tunis and Bizerta have fallen and what remains of the axis is cooped up in the mountains opposite our posn. and in the C. Bon peninsula. We pulled out of the line last night and tomorrow start a 450 miles drive to the Philipville area via Kairouan, Sbeitla, and Tebessa. To do what nobody knows. The entire div. is going. On night 7 May took over O.P. in pouring rain which persisted all night. Yesterday afternoon we were heavily mortared. I fired back but ineffectively. They were very hard to locate. A. has come back. I am still Comd. E. Tp, but don't expect for much longer. The B.C. gets on my nerves. As a matter of fact so does everybody else. Lettercard (23 Ap.) from Dad yesterday. Wrote recently to Pam, B., and Debroy from whom I heard a day or two ago. Very hot. I am sweating profusely. Move at 0615 tomorrow.

Does this move near Algiers presage Com. Op. training and an attack on Sicily I wonder?

Very hot. I am sweating profusely.

From Field of Fire: Diary of a Gunner Officer, *Jack Swaab; Sutton Publishing, 2005.*

Kenneth Morris and HQ Squadron, 4th Armoured Brigade

Crossed from North Africa with the 8th Army to take part in the Allied invasion of Italy in 1943.

We docked at Syracuse in Sicily on 7 August [1943], D Day +28 as planned. Our arrival was greeted by a swarm of bumboats offering for sale pears, grapes and tomatoes. As we were without our transport, we were faced with a five mile march wearing full equipment, haversack, water bottle and respirator, along very dusty roads to a transit camp....

The transit camp had some interesting features. We camped in a large grove of lemon trees next to an extensive vineyard... Little irrigation aqueducts in raised channels surrounded and separated the fields and were widely used by the troops, unhygienically, for washing. Mosquitoes were a problem and had to be countered with tablets, cream and bush nets as protection. Undressing under a bush net was quite awkward, so over the next months many troops succumbed to malaria.

The Allies had a curious relationship with the local population. Although Mussolini had fallen from power on 25 July, technically we were still at war with Italy. The Germans however had not been popular with their Axis partners, requisitioning local food supplies as if they were occupying forces. Islanders regarded themselves as Sicilians rather than Italians. All they wanted was peace. The Allies were thus largely welcomed as liberators.

Report document Morris K. W., 87/44/1 in the Documents Department of the Imperial War Museum.

Captain Harry Butcher, General Eisenhower's naval aide

Describes the tense atmosphere at Ike's headquarters in Malta on Saturday, 10 July 1943, D-Day for the landings in Sicily, which began the Allied move into Europe.

As nothing was expected until around 3 o'clock, I left word for a 'shake' at 2. Whiteley and I were sleeping on light cots in the office of the U.S. Naval Liaison Officer, Commander Boit. I dressed at 2, went to the war room, found there was no news, so went back to my cot.... Didn't want to awaken Ike, who was sleeping soundly in the adjoining room, unless the news warranted it.... About 4.30 Henderson rang to say there had been intercepts of radio signals of the American landing parties to the west, indicating our parties were ashore on Red and Orange beaches, but this didn't mean much.

So didn't bother Ike.... Dozed again, picturing the seasick lads in landing craft and some possibly ashore, and wishing them luck. Ike had rubbed his lucky coins before retiring.

...the 'situation' as of 9.15 a.m. Most paratroopers had landed within one mile of their designated spot. One group hit about ten miles off the target, but even this may further distract the enemy. No report from the gliders, except that six from one were rescued at sea, having failed to glide to land.

No report of any losses of ships.

Getting their information from intercepts of the landing parties' wireless messages, the Royal Navy had numerous fragmentary reports about 5 this morning. The Canadians apparently had not only got ashore, but had their landing craft for tanks beached for unloading. Ships were riding at anchor. The swell had receded.

First fighter sweep from Malta had returned about the time we stirred, and had shot down two Ju-88s....

Nothing is so agonizing as to sit and wait. Now we know how our wives feel when we are late getting home and they don't know where the hell we are.

Since I typed the above, the Royal Navy Signal Officer, Commander L. G. Durlacher, phoned me to say he had a signal from Admiral Hewitt. It said landings at Gela (1st Division) had been made at 2.45, on schedule, followed by succeeding waves of landings. No enemy action of surface ships. No enemy air action. No mines. Slight opposition from the shore. As they approached they could see from the Monrovia that there were many fires in and around Gela, presumably the result of our bombing. The 1st Division... have taken Gela, Hewitt indicated. ...When I told Ike he was elated.

Nothing is so agonizing as to sit and wait.

From Three Years with Eisenhower, *Captain Harry C. Butcher, USNR; William Heinemann, 1946. Originally published in New York by Simon and Schuster.*

Jack Swaab

And so the 51st Highland Division landed in Sicily on D-Day + 1, 11 July 1943, as recorded in the diary kept by gunner officer, Jack Swaab.

12 July

Last night when I lay down under the stars, it was exactly 39 hours since I had slept at all. But I should begin at the beginning. Firstly there was an abrupt break in this narrative because we ran on July 10 into a rolling sea, and our flat bottomed L.S.T. [Landing Ship Tank] rolled so badly that by 1030 I was heartily and decisively sick. This process repeated itself at fairly regular intervals until 1700 when, fully dressed, I fell into an exhausted sleep until 6 the next morning. At about midday, unmolested by aircraft or submarines, we sighted the sandy beach which we knew to be our destination. On the right was a rocky promontory and a lighthouse and the sea was filled, it seemed, with ships. Ships of all shapes and sizes, all colours. L.S.T.s lurching and swaying, slim M.L.s [Mine Layers] almost invisible among the white-capped waves, destroyers, the odd cruiser and over on our left, bringing the Canadians from home, several large liners. We beached about 1300 about 30 yards out and our Jeep (myself at the helm) ploughed gallantly ashore in nearly 3 feet of water. The performance was somewhat dimmed by its giving up the ghost about 500 yards inland; but we got it going again…

At about 2100 the enemy came over and did quite a bit of bombing by flares. In the moonlight and the yellowish glare you could see columns of smoke rising and hear the vicious 'sneezing' of the bombs.

In the harbour, the L.S.T.s lay bulky and silent waiting to beach. The flak was terrific; absolute streams of red Bofors shells and occasionally an Oerlikon gun from one of the ships squirted a necklace of white cannon bullets. The battery came off into the rocky shallows about 2200, formed up a couple of miles inland for de-waterproofing and at 0245 recce parties moved off in the dark in a cold mist....

Very slight enemy air activity – the R.A.F. are giving us wonderful cover. I slept like the dead for 9 hours last night. Everybody rather cheerful and optimistic; certainly less opposition than expected has been met. We are 8th army again thank the Lord, and under Monty who was seen yesterday in a Duck on our front.

. . . our Jeep (myself at the helm) ploughed gallantly ashore in nearly 3 feet of water.

From Field of Fire, *Jack Swaab; Sutton Publishing, 2005.*

Kenneth Morris

'Monty' seems to confirm rumours among Kenneth Morris's brigade that the 8th Army's next theatre of war is going to be much nearer home than Italy.

On 9 October [1943] Brigade HQ paraded for an informal visit by General Montgomery. In part this was recompense for a spit-and-polish parade on 1 September when he failed to appear.... He bestowed a few medals... [and] afterwards addressed the troops, gathered round in his familiar pattern.

He was heard with great interest...[By] now it seemed likely that some British troops would be withdrawn from Italy to prepare for the second front. And from 30 September troops had been forbidden to use the cable code for 'May see you soon'.

Montgomery ... did not disappoint. After stressing the value of Eighth Army's team spirit and esprit de corps, he said that, when his job in hand had been completed, he wanted the original units of his desert army to follow him, whether to India or China (at which faces lengthened) or even to England (relief). That did little to damp down speculation or rumour...

Montgomery ... did not disappoint.

Report document Morris, K. W., 87/44/1 in the Documents Department of the Imperial War Museum.

Mike Austin-Smith

How an officer in the Royal Horse Artillery survived the fourth and last phase of the five-month long Battle of Monte Cassino, which cleared the way for the Allies to advance on Rome.

21 May 1944

I crossed over the river a week ago today and went into the fun in support of our own Lancers… Well, the first day was pretty sticky with the bridge head only a few thousand yards deep, in places much less, every square inch was under shell or mortar fire. The first day I think we had more shelling than in the whole of North Africa. Things were a bit shambolic, with no coordinated plan, and we sat on a ridge for about 5 hours and they dished it out solid. It was extremely hot inside the tank, it was red hot and we were simply pouring with perspiration, and drinking water as hard as we could go. That night when we leaguered we had Nebelwerfers and mortars dropping in the leaguer so no echelon could get to us and we had to sleep in the tank. This we thought a bit rough but we managed it and were grateful for its protection when during the night all manner of shellfire came down. Well, each day has been very similar and lots of shelling, but each day we pushed on steadily under terrific barrages with tanks and infantry and each day it eased a little until finally he broke and we rumbled straight on to the Hitler Line defensive position. . .

From Life, Love and War: Letters Home 1939-1946, *by Mike Austin-Smith; privately printed.*

Howard Connor, official historian of the V Marine Corps

Tells of the horrors of the first day of the assault by 8,000 US marines on the strategically important Japanese island fortress of Iwo Jima, 19 February 1945.

Wounded men were arriving on the beach by the dozen, where they were not much better off than they had been at the front.... The first two boats bringing in badly needed litters were blown out of the water. Casualties were being hit again as they lay helpless under blankets awaiting evacuation.

> The first two boats bringing in badly needed litters were blown out of the water.

From The World at Arms: The Reader's Digest Illustrated History of World War II; *Reader's Digest Association, 1989.*

THE WAR IN THE AIR

The War in the Air

Aeroplanes, like the tank, were seen as an extra aid for traditional land forces at the outbreak of war in 1914. By the end of World War I, when Britain's Royal Flying Corps had been renamed the Royal Air Force, aircraft were on their way to becoming the basis of a separate branch of warfare. True, the United States waited until after World War II was over to rename the USAAF (United States Army Air Force) the USAF (United States Air Force). But the USA returned to an isolationist position after 1918, remained neutral in 1939, and did not enter the war until it had been going for more than two years.

The Royal Air Force was essential to the success of the British land forces, both at home and in Africa, Europe, Asia and the Far East, and to its navy, where the Fleet Air Arm, part of the RAF operating within the Royal Navy, was both protector of the ships of the merchant navy and an attacker. On its own, the RAF also fought a war in the air against a single enemy, the German Luftwaffe.

In the months after the declaration of war in September 1939, not a lot happened on land or in the air, as far as Britain was concerned. At sea, it was a very different matter. In the Atlantic, the fighter planes of the Fleet Air Arm, operating from the flight decks of aircraft carriers, played a large part in seeking out and destroying the German U-boats and surface warships that were taking such a huge toll of the vital convoys bringing essential food and supplies into the North Atlantic from Canada and the United States and from as far away as Australia and New Zealand.

The saving of the British Expeditionary Force from the beaches of Dunkirk in May 1940 involved the RAF to a lesser extent than it did the Royal Navy, but it was still vitally important. The RAF came out of the air battles rather better than the Luftwaffe, despite the experience the latter had gained fighting for Franco in the Spanish Civil War. The RAF lost 930 planes, nearly half of them fighters, in the air battles over Belgium and France in 1940, while the Luftwaffe lost nearly 1,300 aircraft.

Those fighter planes lost by the RAF could have cost the country dear during the Battle of Britain in the summer of 1940, when the Luftwaffe threw everything it could at the RAF's Fighter Command. Many of the young men who flew the Hurricanes and Spitfires that won the Battle of Britain came from Australia, Canada, New Zealand and South Africa, whose countries had declared war on Germany within days of 3 September. There were also many young Polish air force men, who had managed to escape from Poland after the German invasion, and even Americans, anxious to get in on the action and soon formed into their own Eagle Squadrons. The battles in the air over Britain in August and September 1940 were fought over the heads and within sight of the inhabitants of the towns and villages, farms and industrial sites below. Both the Battle of Britain and the Blitz which followed it were military campaigns fought entirely in the air – an historic first for world warfare.

During the Battle of Britain, a German bomber pilot dropped his bomb load over London, not to attack the capital so much as to lighten his load for the flight home. Winston Churchill, incensed at this attack on the civilian population, ordered a reprisal bombing on Berlin. Hitler, in turn, decided to start bombing Britain's capital and its industrial cities as well as the airfields, merchant convoys at sea and ports that had been the Luftwaffe's main targets so far. Thus the Blitz began.

The Battle of Britain over, the RAF's fighter crews, although still with much to do in the skies over Britain, were also now flying much further afield, first of all guarding the planes of Bomber Command, now in full attack mode on German-occupied Europe, then on over the deserts of North Africa, and beyond to South-East Asia and the Far East.

The United States of America was brought into the war as the result of an air attack – Japan's attack on its Pacific Fleet in Pearl Harbor. The USAAF, while heavily involved in the air war against Germany and Italy in Europe and North Africa, was also the main combatant in the air war against Japan in the Pacific, in the Philippines and the Far East. It was from a USAAF B-29 bomber, piloted by Lt.-Colonel Paul Tibbets, that the first atomic bomb was dropped in war – on the Japanese city of Hiroshima on 6 August 1945.

Sam Hall

New Zealander Sam Hall survived his time as a navigator with RAF Bomber Command in England.

In 1937 I had already joined the 1st Battalion of the Wellington Regiment, and so by 1939 I was a well-trained heavy machine-gunner. When the war started I had no desire to carry a 47 pound machine-gun with me wherever I went.... I thought it would be a much more comfortable war sitting down.... I had to wait until the RNZAF announced its recruiting scheme, an intake of 20 pilots, 20 observers and 20 air gunners every month. That morning I went in one door of the bank in which I worked, the Bank of New Zealand, signed in the attendance book and ran out the other door of the bank to the Air Department to sign on. I found that I would have to wait a whole year before I could become a pilot, but a friend in the Air Department said that if I was prepared to sign on as an observer he would put my file on the top. I was in in a month.

The instructors were well-trained experienced officers, mainly from the RAF, but they had so little equipment... We flew for navigation in the small airliners of Union Airways, DH 86s and 89s, and when I left New Zealand as a fully trained observer I'd done a total of 52 hours flying. Four of them were at night over New Zealand with lights on, and yet I was destined for Bomber Command.

From Bomber Command 1939-45, *Richard Overy; HarperCollins Publishers, 1997.*

Spitfire pilot Flight Lieutenant David Crook D.F.C.

Describes in Spitfire Pilot *a personally frustrating but successful day's work for 609 Squadron in 'the lull before the storm' in early August 1940.*

On 8th August [1940], soon after dawn, we were ordered to patrol a convoy off the Needles. It was a very clear day with a brilliant sun – just the sort of days the Germans love, because they come out at a very big height and dive down to attack out of the sun.... [The] convoy was a big one and escorted by several destroyers and balloons towed from barges in order to stop low-flying dive-bombing....

We steered out towards the convoy, which was now about twelve miles south of Bournemouth. There was a small layer of cloud, and while dodging in and out of this... I glanced out towards the convoy, and saw three of the balloons falling in flames. Obviously an attack was starting, and I climbed above the cloud layer and went towards the convoy at full throttle, climbing all the time towards the sun, so that I could deliver my attack with the sun behind me.

I was now about five miles from the convoy, and could see a big number of enemy fighters circling above, looking exactly like a swarm of flies buzzing round a pot of jam. Below them the dive-bombers were diving down on the ships and great fountains of white foam were springing up where their bombs struck the water. I could see that one or two ships had already been hit and were on fire.

I saw several machines diving down with smoke and flame pouring out of them, and then I spotted an Me109 flying about 4,000 feet below me. I immediately turned and dived down on him – he was a sitting target, but before I got to him a Hurricane appeared and shot him down in flames. I was annoyed....

[I] landed back at base, to find everybody safely back. The C.O., Michael, and John had each destroyed an Me109, while Mac had shot down two Junkers 87 dive-bombers.

Obviously an attack was starting, and I climbed above the cloud layer and went towards the convoy at full throttle, climbing all the time towards the sun . . .

From Spitfire Pilot: A Personal Account of the Battle of Britain, Flight Lieutenant D. M. Crook, D.F.C.; 1st published, Faber, 1942, new edition, Grub Street, London, 2008.

Kenneth Gundry, a pilot officer in 257 Squadron

Describing in a letter to his parents his part in the massive Eagle Day action, launched by the Luftwaffe on 13 August 1940.

We separated as a flight and found ourselves sitting under about eighty Me110 fighters milling around in a huge circle. Above them were about fifty or more Me109s. Two of our five got split away by a few stray Jerries buzzing around and then the next thing I knew was a ruddy great earthquake in my A/C [aircraft] and my control column was almost solid. On my left another Hurricane was floating about over a complex network of smoke trails left by cannon shells and incendiary. We had been attacked by another unseen bunch of Me110s... I joined up with another Hurricane and Jerry just seemed to dissolve. We just couldn't find any at all.

> Two of our five got split away by a few stray Jerries buzzing around and then the next thing I knew ...

Quoted in Fighter Boys, *by Patrick Bishop; Harper Collins, 2003.*

Spitfire pilot Flight Lieutenant David Crook of 609 Squadron

Crook describes what RAF's Spitfire and Hurricane squadrons were up against during the Battle of Britain. David Crook was killed in 1944. A Spitfire he flew with 609 Squadron is now in the Imperial War Museum in London.

A powerful force of German aircraft was circling over the east end of the Isle of Wight, and I went out towards them, climbing all the time. As I got nearer, I was staggered by the number of Huns in the sky. I think we had always imagined that raids might be carried out by three or four squadrons at most – some forty or fifty aircraft.

And here, circling and sweeping all over the sky, were at least 200 Huns! 'My God,' I muttered to myself, 'What a party.' I was not the only person to be impressed. Several other people (not only in 609) who were also in this fight told me afterwards that their main impression had been one of blank astonishment at the numbers of aircraft involved. – 'There was the whole German Air Force, bar Goering.' Later in the summer we got used to seeing these enormous formations, but this first occasion certainly made us think a bit.

I climbed out towards the Huns and saw three formations of Messerschmitts circling round, one above the other, between 20,000 and 28,000 feet. Each layer had formed into the usual German defensive circle, going round and round on each other's tails. I decided to attack the middle layer, which was composed of Me110s . . .

From Spitfire Pilot: A Personal Account of the Battle of Britain, *Flight Lieutenant D. M. Crook, D.F.C.; 1st published, Faber, 1942, new edition, Grub Street, London, 2008.*

British fighter pilot Richard Hillary

Young and handsome, Richard Hillary was not to be so lucky later. Shot down in flames, he spent many months in Sir Archibald McIndoe's East Grinstead plastic-surgery hospital being given a new face. His book, The Last Enemy, *from which this quote is taken, became a classic of World War II flying literature.*

The voice of the controller came unhurried over the loud-speaker, telling us to take off, and in a few seconds we were running for our machines. I climbed into the cockpit of my plane and felt an empty sensation of suspense in the pit of my stomach.... I knew that that morning I was to kill for the first time. That I might be killed or in any way injured did not occur to me.

We ran into them at 18,000 feet, twenty yellow-nosed Messerschmitt 109s, about 500 feet above us. Our Squadron strength was eight, and as they came down on us we went into line astern and turned head on to them. Brian Carbury, who was leading the section, dropped the nose of his machine, and I could almost feel the leading Nazi pilot push forward on his stick to bring his guns to bear. At the same moment, Brian hauled back hard on his own control stick and led us over them in a steep climbing turn to the left. In two vital seconds they had lost their advantage. I saw Brian let go a burst of fire at the leading plane, saw the pilot put his machine into a half roll, and knew that he was mine. Automatically, I kicked the rudder to the left to get him at right angles, turned the gun-button to 'Fire' and let go in a four-second burst with full deflection. He came right through my sights and I saw the tracer from all eight guns thud home. For a second he seemed to hang motionless, then a jet of red flame shot upwards and he spun out of sight....

It had happened.

My first emotion was one of satisfaction, satisfaction at a job adequately done, at the final logical conclusion of months of specialized training. And then I had a feeling of the essential rightness of it all. He was dead and I was alive; it could so easily have been the other way round....

Automatically, I kicked the rudder to the left to get him at right angles, turned the gun-button to 'Fire' and let go in a four-second burst with full deflection.

From The Last Enemy, *Richard Hillary; Burford Books, 1942.*

George Bennions, a sergeant pilot in 41 Squadron

George Bennions was badly burnt when bailing out of his burning Spitfire during the Battle of Britain. He was operated on by the plastic surgeon Sir Archibald McIndoe.

...there were just two holes in his face.

[I] was on crutches at the time [in Queen Victoria Hospital, East Grinstead] but I managed to get over [to Ward 3] with a lot of struggle and self-pity. As I opened the door I saw...the most horrifying thing I have seen in my life. [There] was this chap who had been badly burnt, really badly burnt. His hair was burnt off, his eyebrows were burnt off, his eyelids were burnt off. You could just see his staring eyes. His nose was burnt, there were just two holes in his face. His lips were badly burnt. Then, when I looked down his hands were burnt... his feet were burnt. This chap started propelling a wheelchair down the ward. Half-way down he picked up a chair with his teeth. Then he brought this chair down the ward, threw it alongside me and said: 'Have a seat, old boy.' I cried. I thought, 'What have I got to complain about?'

Quoted in Fighter Boys, *by Patrick Bishop; Harper Collins, 2003.*

Nancy Mullet, Women's Auxiliary Air Force

Once she was in, Nancy Mullet spent four years in the Women's Auxiliary Air Force, managing to fit in marriage to her sweetheart Ralph Walton when they both had leave in September 1945.

My reasons for joining the WAAF are vague, even to me. In mid-1941 a friend with whom I worked and I just decided that we would do so. I can only think that we were bored and wanted to do something different, and we did have a vague idea that we could release an airman for active service. We tried to get into the WAAF but were told that recruiting was closed...

We then tried the ATS, but were unable to get into this service, probably because of our work at the Food Office. By the beginning of 1942 recruitment in the WAAF restarted and we tried again to enter that service. We had told our employer that we wished to join and for my job they engaged two additional people – a clerk and a shorthand typist. (The job had been growing with the increasing amount of rationing and food control.) However, we were told by the WAAF that we still could not be released but that they would send our names for 'special screening'. I have never been sure whether our enlistment was due to this special screening or to the fact that female conscription was introduced about this time, which might have made it difficult for employers to retain staff.

File document Mrs. N. C. Walton, 88/2/1 in the Documents Department of the Imperial War Museum.

Subaltern Ian Bell

A water supply engineer with the Royal Engineers in the Western Desert, Ian Bell had been captured when he witnessed this battle royal in the air over his prisoner-of-war camp in May 1942.

One of the boys pointed to a few specks in the sky fairly high up and as their engines roared louder and louder, we found the specks to be our own aircraft. ... The show started about 9.30 a.m., when a 'Kitty-Hawk' hedge-hopped over the transports, loosing off its cannons and heavy machine guns, dropping a 250lb bomb plumb on to a Boche anti-aircraft gun-carrier, smashing it to bits.

No sooner had one 'plane flown around creating havoc than another would appear. All were doing their utmost to destroy the German armour and transports. The burst from the ack-ack guns were terrific. Every German and Italian used his rifle or tommy-gun and with the loud cracking 20 m.m. quick-firing ack-ack guns popping off just nearby, the noise was frightful....

About mid-day, a flock of twelve 'Stukas' came flying low, straight for the camp. The Boche thought they were our 'planes and opened up at them with everything they had.... Little did [the Stukas] realise that our 'Kitty-Hawks' were sitting above them. The Kittys waited until the twelve Stukas were right over the centre of the camp and then they dived down for the kill and to give Rommel a real show.

In the space of a few seconds, two Stukas were biting the dust and ending their careers in flames. Most of the boys were sitting up now and cheering away just as they would at a soccer match back home.... The Kittys were diving in and out of the showers of bullets that were flung up at them, for they were very fast and most manoeuvrable.

Down went another Stuka! Then the shouts and pointings of the fellows drew my gaze upwards. My heart beat faster as I counted eight Messerschmitt 109s preparing to pounce on our game little Kittys. They dived down from their great height, only to be outmanoeuvred. The ensuing dog-fight was a thrill to watch....

Particularly interesting was one fight between a 109 and a Kitty. The latter was completing a circuit of the camp just after shooting down its fifth Stuka [all twelve Stukas were finally shot down]. The pilot suddenly saw he was being chased by the 109. It was incredible to watch the 109 catch up with the Kitty in a matter of seconds, until suddenly our machine climbed almost vertically. The 109 roared past as the skilful Kitty pilot half-rolled at the top of his climb and screamed down on his victim from out of the sun. The surprise was complete. A burst of fire went straight into the side of the 109, tearing off a wing. Swinging crazily for a second, the enemy plane crashed to earth.

I tried to cheer but my throat had long since seized up. The Kitty flew once more round the camp, completely ignoring the ack-ack. As he flew over our heads, he 'shot us up' and waggled Kitty's wings – as if to say 'O.K. chaps, we know you are there'.

File document Bell, R. I., 87/34/1 in the Documents Department of the Imperial War Museum.

Fitzroy Maclean

Describes some very effective air camouflage in the Western Desert.

Our first care when we halted was to camouflage our trucks against observation from the air. We usually chose as a stopping-place a dip in the ground, or some rocks, or a patch of scrub. Carefully disposing our vehicles so as to make the best use of such cover as there was, we would then set about blending them in to the background, with bits of scrub and camouflage nets stretched right over them. The L.R.D.G. [Long Range Desert Group] trucks were painted with a bold design of rose-pink and olive-green, which, oddly enough, made them practically invisible against the desert. Later the S.A.S. adopted the same camouflage, and several times I was caught in the open by low-flying enemy aircraft without the pilot seeming to notice us.

. . . we would then set about blending them in to the background, with bits of scrub and camouflage nets . . .

From Eastern Approaches, *Fitzroy Maclean; Jonathan Cape, 1949.*

Denholm Elliott

Young acting hopeful Denholm Elliott was in a Halifax bomber that ditched in the North Sea while on a bombing raid in September 1942. He and four other survivors of the bomber's seven-man crew were picked up by a tug and taken ashore, to become prisoners-of-war until 1945.

As we were walking out to the plane the engineer who had been servicing it said 'What are you?' I said 'I'm wireless op for K for King.' He said 'Oh dear, oh dear,' and I asked 'Why?' 'Well the last wireless operator for K for King got a cannon shell up his backside.'...

This was the first time I was actually encountering anti-aircraft fire [1,000 feet over the target, a submarine base] and it really was a most unpleasant sensation. A shell bursting beneath you lifts the plane about fifty feet upwards in the air. You certainly find instant religion....

[Then I] felt the most enormous explosion... the port outer engine was on fire... all the lights went out. I was fumbling desperately to find the wire clippers to send a distress signal on the automatic SOS but the plane was going down and there just wasn't time. I just jumped out of my seat which was at the very front of the plane and tore to the middle of the aircraft, as it was going down, and got into the ditching position with your feet up against the central spar and your hands behind your neck to take the shock. [The navigator] sort of grinned in a sickly way... that was the last I saw of him.

File document Denholm Elliott, 98/7/1 in the Documents Department of the Imperial War Museum.

Alexander Pokryshkin

Alexander Pokryshkin went on to bag another 58 victories, won fighting 137 aerial battles for Russia. He was awarded the title 'Hero of the Soviet Union' three times and received his third Hero's Gold Star Medal in 1944.

I was out with pilot Semyonov as my partner flying on a reconnaissance mission to Jassy where the Germans had an aerodrome. As we approached the town I espied five Messerschmitts flying towards us, three below us and two above. Here, at last, were live Germans. They spotted us. I rocked my wings as a signal to Semyonov that I was going to attack....

I was flying a MiG-3. It is a sturdy machine and well armed. It behaves wonderfully at high altitudes when its speed and manoeuvrability increase. I had my plan of action all worked out in an instant. Semyonov was to cover me as we had previously arranged on the ground. I shot up into the clouds and kept on climbing until I ran into one of the two Messerschmitts coming

The Messerschmitt burst into flames and plunged downwards....

The other German had crept up behind me. White ribbons of his tracers shot by and then my plane shuddered.

towards me. The German zoomed almost in my face. I did a stall-turn and found myself on the tail of the yellow, blunt-winged craft. I fired at short range. The Messerschmitt burst into flames and plunged downwards.... The other German had crept up behind me. White ribbons of his tracers shot by and then my plane shuddered. Its port wing had been torn by bullets. I dived to zero feet and hedge-hopped all the way home... I made a normal landing, taxied to a stop, shut off the engine and slumped against the armoured back of the seat. I needed a drink. My throat was parched. That was the first German I had bagged.

From Handbook of World War II, *Karen Farrington; Abbeydale Press, 2008; orig. ed. Bookmart Ltd, 2001.*

Richard Dimbleby

Reporter Richard Dimbleby describes for BBC listeners an attack on Berlin by 106 Squadron of Bomber Command in January 1943. Dimbleby accompanied Wing Commander Guy Gibson's crew on the long raid.

There was a complete ring of powerful searchlights, waving and crossing. Though it seemed to me that when many of our bombers were over the city, many of our lights were doused. There was also intense flak. First of all they didn't seem to be aiming at us. It was bursting away to starboard and away to port in thick yellow clusters and dark, smoky puffs. As we turned in for our first run across the city it closed right around us. For a moment it seemed impossible that we could miss it. And one burst lifted us in the air as if a giant hand had pushed up the belly of the machine. But we flew on, and just then another Lancaster dropped a load of incendiaries. And where a moment before there had been a dark patch of the city, a dazzling silver pattern spread itself. A rectangle of brilliant lights, hundreds, thousands of them, winking and gleaming and lighting the outlines of the city around them. As though this

At last our bomb-aimer sighted his objective below, and for one unpleasant minute we flew steady and straight.

unloading had been the signal, score after score of fire bombs went down and all over the dark face of the German capital these great incandescent flowerbeds spread themselves.... We flew over the city three times for more than half an hour while the guns sought us out and failed to hit us. At last our bomb-aimer sighted his objective below, and for one unpleasant minute we flew steady and straight. Then he pressed the button and the biggest bomb of the evening, our three-and-a-half-tonner fell away and down.

File 2162 in the Imperial War Museum sound archive; quoted in Bomber Boys, *Patrick Bishop; Harper Perennial, 2008.*

Patrick Bishop

With the help of Squadron Leader Tony Iveson DFC, who took part in the attack, Patrick Bishop describes in Bomber Boys *how the* Tirpitz *was sunk.*

On 12 November [1944] they tried again. The thirty Lancasters of 9 and 617 squadrons that mounted the attack [on the *Tirpitz*] had been specially modified so as to be able to reach Tromsø from Lossiemouth.... All armour plating as well as the mid-upper and front gun turrets were removed. They were also fitted with improved-performance Merlin T24 engines. Loaded with a [1,200-pound] Tallboy, they were just capable of making the twelve-and-a-half hour round trip.

Tony Iveson and seventeen other 617 Squadron crews were set to take off at 2 a.m. They lined up while the hoarfrost was swept from the wings then 'off we went, up past the Orkneys and the Shetlands to about 65 north, seven east, when we turned towards Norway'.... As morning broke 'it was absolutely gin clear. You could see for miles and below the white-topped mountains the blue, blue sea.'...

When they arrived, the *Tirpitz* appeared to have been taken by surprise. There was no smoke screen. It

After the fourteenth bomb they weren't able to plot any more because there was so much smoke and muck around.

was Sunday and many of the crew were ashore. Iveson and the rest of 617 Squadron dropped their bombs within the space of four minutes from 15,000 feet. Their Lancasters were fitted with a new, computer-assisted bombsight. The Tallboys fell away on a beautiful steady course. After the fourteenth bomb they weren't able to plot any more because there was so much smoke and muck around. The accuracy was extraordinary. There were two direct hits on the battleship and three near misses. Within six minutes of the first strike she was on her side. Within eleven minutes she had capsized but was unable to sink completely because of the shallowness of the water. Nearly a thousand sailors were killed or injured out of the ship's company of 1,900 men, including the captain and most of the officers.

File 2162 in the Imperial War Museum sound archive; quoted in Bomber Boys, *Patrick Bishop; Harper Perennial, 2008.*

Lieutenant David H. Rust, a P-40 pilot with the USAAF's 23rd Fighter Group's 75th Fighter Squadron in China

Describes some spectacular aerobatics during a fight with two Japanese planes in 1944.

Soon I picked up a couple of… Jap Oscars and went after them hammer and tongs, using War Emergency power once more. Each time I rammed that throttle through the gate, it was an awesome experience. The big Allison [V-1710-39 1,150 hp engine] would bellow and press you back in the seat, the engine cowling actually seemed to swell with power, and the black smoke rolled. One of the Oscars broke away but I stayed with the other one and even followed him through some violent manoeuvring. This, plus the essential glances over my own tail, occupied my total attention. Though I didn't realise it at that moment, I actually lost track of where the ground was. I was closing in on my Jap, and had just begun firing at a relatively favourable range and angle-off, when to my astonishment and alarm, the horizon hove into view – upside down! I had committed one of the major no-no's in letting this Jap lead me into a loop. But I stayed on my target as long as I could, getting a number of visible hits on his fuselage.

Slowed down as we were, he was able to pull a tighter loop than I could, so I had to break off. Knowing I was vulnerable at that point, I went right into the Chennault manoeuvre, stick and rudder full right and forward. The airplane threw me against the seat belt, going around an outside barrel roll straight down. I stayed in it for a few seconds, but couldn't see anybody behind me and pulled out, bringing the throttle back to max. continuous and starting another high speed climb with my eyes scanning the sky with increasing urgency. I saw two fires burning below; but no planes at all.

I was closing in on my Jap, and had just begun firing at a relatively favourable range and angle-off, when to my astonishment and alarm, the horizon hove into view – upside down!

From USAAF Handbook 1939-1945, *Martin W. Bowman; Sutton Publishing, 1997.*

Wildcat pilot Norman Sargent of 835 Naval Air Squadron

Recalls a distinctly hairy landing on the bucking flight-deck of the carrier Nairana, *on convoy escort duty in the Arctic, during a violent storm in February 1945.*

Rebounding from the barrier, I slithered across the deck on my wingtip. First I was almost blown [by the seventy-knot wind] over the starboard side, then I was almost blown over the round-down. Much to their credit, a lot of the flight-deck handling party tried to grab me as I slithered past them; but they hadn't a hope of stopping five tons of fast-moving Wildcat. I rammed open my throttle, managed to stop the glissade, and came to rest no more than a dozen feet from the round-down. From here I was hauled to safety.

. . . I slithered across the deck on my wingtip.

From Alone on a Wide, Wide Sea, *E. E. Barringer; Leo Cooper, 1995.*

THE WAR AT SEA

The War at Sea

The navies of Great Britain, Germany, Italy, Japan and the United States of America were the main contenders in the war at sea during World War II. They fought in three great seas, the Atlantic and Pacific oceans and the Mediterranean. In 1939 Britain's Royal Navy was the world's largest navy and its merchant fleet was also the biggest in the world.

In 1939 the leaders of the world's navies had not yet fully accepted that much had changed about war at sea since World War I. Success no longer depended on the size and firepower of warships alone; aircraft, particularly when operating from the decks of ships far from land, would now have the greatest say in any navy's success,

especially when armed with bombs and torpedoes capable of penetrating the heaviest armour-plating.

Events at sea in the first days and weeks of the war obscured this basic truth. Just one day after war was declared, a British liner, *Athenia*, was sunk by a German U-boat off Ireland, with the loss of more than 200 lives, including 28 American. By the end of September, U-boats, of which there were 159 in the German navy at the start of the war, had accounted for 20 British ships in the Atlantic, including a warship, HMS *Courageous*. In October, a U-boat penetrated into Scapa Flow, the 'safe' Royal Navy anchorage in the Orkneys, and attacked the ships there, sinking the *Royal Oak* and leaving 600 sailors dead.

The greatest success that the Royal Navy could point to in reply in the early months of the war was the Battle of the River Plate in December 1939. This resulted in the German pocket battleship, *Admiral Graf Spee*, badly damaged in an encounter with the heavy cruiser, HMS *Exeter* and the two light cruisers, the Royal Navy's *Ajax* and New Zealand's *Achilles*, being scuttled in Montevideo Harbour. And it was possible to see the magnificent role played by the Royal Navy and an extraordinary fleet of civilian craft at Dunkirk in May/June 1940 as a sort of victory.

The first years of the war in the Atlantic confirmed both that the initial successes of the German U-boat fleet were not just good fortune and that heavy warships were vulnerable. U-boats accounted for hundreds of thousands of tons of shipping and their vital cargoes in the merchant convoys of the Atlantic and the Mediterranean in 1940 and 1941 and, after Russia became an ally in 1941, on the Arctic convoys to Murmansk. At the same time, a heavy toll on large warships, notably HMS *Hood* and the mighty German battleship *Bismarck* in the Atlantic in May 1941, and the aircraft carrier *Ark Royal* in the Mediterranean later that year, underlined their vulnerability.

The balance of power in the Atlantic changed when the Royal Navy was able to add to its possession of radar an ability to break the codes used by the German navy for its radio signals. The entry of America into the war in 1941 also made a great difference in the Atlantic, where their Liberty ships did a magnificent job helping the Royal Navy, especially its corvettes, protect hundreds of merchant convoys. By late 1943, the U-boat threat in the Atlantic had been neutralised.

At the start of the war, the Allies were unopposed in the Mediterranean, allowing oil from the Middle East to come safely through the Suez Canal. The entry of Italy into the war as an Axis power changed this. Their navy was modern and large, and the close proximity of land bases for aircraft meant that its lack of an aircraft carrier was not a problem. An early, 'hateful' decision that had to be made as a result of the entry of Italy into the war was the destruction of the French fleet at its base near Oran in Algeria to keep it out of Axis hands.

The Royal Navy early gained the upper hand over its Italian opponent. An attack by Swordfish from the aircraft carrier *Illustrious* on the Italian fleet in the port of Taranto in November 1940 seriously damaged three Italian battleships. At Cape Matapan, in Greece, in March 1941 the Royal Navy proved wrong Mussolini's boast that he would make the Mediterranean an 'Italian lake', destroying five Italian ships and damaging others, while 2,400 Italian seamen lost their lives.

The shallow waters of the Mediterranean were more difficult than the Atlantic for U-boats to operate in, since they could be spotted from the air even when submerged. Nevertheless, it was U-boat torpedoes that sank the *Ark Royal* and U-boats, as well as surface ships, did much damage – though not as much as Germany's Stukas and seaplanes – to the convoys to Malta and to besieged Tobruk before the port fell to the Germans in December 1941.

The war in the Pacific was very much an American war, with US Pacific-based fleets covering thousands of miles of the Pacific Ocean, the South China Sea and the Philippine Sea during their mighty tussle with Japan. Several major sea battles between the two powers included the American-won battles of Midway, Coral Sea and Leyte Gulf. Fought over three days in October 1944 over an area of the Pacific the size of France, Leyte Gulf was the decisive battle of the war, securing the Philippines for the Allies.

For US marines, the war in the Pacific involved heavily-contested landings on islands from the Solomon and Marshall Islands to the Marianas and the volcanic island of Iwo Jima. The battle for Iwo Jima in February 1945 was one of the fiercest and the most heroic in the US Marine Corps' history; it was also one of the most strategically important, for it helped clear the way to the heart of Japan.

Lieutenant A. Dann

A naval officer who crossed the Channel to Dunkirk with the first convoy of small boats, was introduced to this motley armada at Sheerness.

The first assembly was typical of the whole of this miniature armada. A dozen or so motor yachts from 20 to 50 feet in length, nicely equipped and smartly maintained by proud individual owners, a cluster of 'cheap' conversion jobs mainly the work of amateur craftsmen, who had set to work in their spare time to convert a ship's lifeboat or any old half discarded hull into a cabin cruiser of sorts… and half a dozen Thames river launches resembling nothing so much as the upper decks of elongated motor buses with their rows of slatted seats, but given a tang of the waterside by rows of painted lifebuoys slung around the upper sails…. A strange flotilla indeed to be taking an active part in what has been described as the greatest naval epic in history.

> A strange flotilla indeed to be taking an active part …

From Dann's Report in the National Archives; quoted in Dunkirk: Fight to the Last Man, *Hugh Sebag-Montefiore; Penguin Books, 2007.*

Rear-Admiral William Wake-Walker

In charge of shipping off Dunkirk, describes a heart-lifting sight in the early evening of 31 May 1940.

I saw for the first time that strange procession of craft of all kinds that has become famous. Tugs towing dinghies, lifeboats and all manner of pulling boats, small motor yachts, motor launches, drifters, Dutch schoots, Thames barges, fishing boats, pleasure steamers…

> Tugs towing dinghies, lifeboats and all manner of pulling boats . . .

From Wake-Walter's Report in the National Archives; quoted in Dunkirk: Fight to the Last Man, *Hugh Sebag-Montefiore; Penguin Books, 2007.*

Major Colvin

The experience of acting commanding officer Major Colvin and his men was all too common during the evacuation from Dunkirk.

After some time, a motor boat towing a chain of empty ships' boats came out to us [on a grounded steamer off Bray-Dunes].… As we neared the destroyer [probably HMS *Keith*, which was sunk later that day] it was attacked… by dive-bombers and hit in the engines. She put to sea as quickly as possible with clouds of smoke pouring from her, and was subsequently abandoned.

> As we neared the destroyer it was attacked … by dive-bombers and hit in the engines.

From Dunkirk: Fight to the Last Man, *Hugh Sebag-Montefiore; Penguin Books, 2007; this quote was taken from* Grenadier Guards in the War, *Forbes.*

Able Seaman Roy Kilburn

Roy Kilburn was one of only three survivors of the sinking of HMS Hood, *the pride of the Royal Navy, by the* Bismarck *and the* Prinz Eugen *in the North Atlantic on 24 May 1941.*

I was a member of the anti-aircraft gun crew but, of course, we weren't needed. There were only two other people with me at the time. The others were in a shelter deck – a shell had gone in there and killed all of them, about 200 men – but I didn't know that at the time. One of the shells hit one of the ready-fuse lockers for the four inch guns and there was a fire on board the upper deck and then there was this terrific explosion. It was most peculiar, the dead silence that followed it – I don't know if we were deaf.

… I went to the ship's side to be sick. I noticed that the ship was rolling over and the bows were coming out of the water so I started taking off my tin hat, gas mask, anti-flash gear, oilskin, so that I would have a chance to swim. With the ship rolling over, I just went into the water and the water came up to me.

I was terrified. I had a small rubber life belt on which you blew up – it was partially blown up. I started swimming away from the ship. The ship rolled over and the yard arms which had been broken during the action hit me across the legs and the wireless aerials tangled round my legs, pulling me down with the ship. I cut my seaboots off with the knife, and shot up, like a cork out of a bottle. The ship was around 10 yards away from me with her bows straight up in the air – and she just sank.

From Handbook of World War II *by Karen Farrington; Abbeydale Press, 2006.*

Naval engine room artificer Clifford Simkin

The Flamingo *took part in the evacuation of Greece from Piraeus in 1941.*

[During April–May 1941] we were operating [in the Blackswan class AA sloop *Flamingo*] from Piraeus. The intense bombing carried on day after day, night after night; after any daytime raid we would anchor but remain ready to get under way for immediate action, then at five minutes before the next raid was due we would lift the hook and wait for the enemy aircraft to come. We knew they would not disappoint us. The orders were full speed ahead and the ship would weave in and out of a group of merchant ships trying to draw the enemy's fire, and at the same time we would be shooting at their aircraft with our three twin four-inch AA guns, a four-barrelled pom-pom, Oerlikons and Lewis guns, at the same time remembering to conserve our fuel and ammunition. By night we would take our chickens [the merchant ships] around the Greek islands and the Germans used to drop tons of bombs, saturating the area, hoping firstly that they would hit some ship, or maybe more, and secondly that we would reply with our guns, giving our position away. It was better to risk being hit in the dark, to keep quiet and save your ammunition.

Report document Simkin, C., 91/17/1 in the Documents Department of the Imperial War Museum.

Leading Seaman Cyril Stephens

Cyril Stephens knew all about the notorious corkscrew motion of the Flower class corvettes when in mid-Atlantic, serving in HMS Orchis *for three years escorting convoys in the Atlantic.*

> # It was all right when you weren't seasick, but when you were seasick it was a different matter.

It was almost as though it was like a terrier shaking a bit of rag. You know the old ship'd wiggle somehow. It'd corkscrew up on top of a wave and you'd be up and you'd look down into this trough and you'd think, crikey, and the next thing you'd be down in there and a bloomin' great wave'd come over the top. It was a challenge somehow. You'd think, crikey, we'll stick this lot out and sometimes it was exhilarating at times, you know, you'd think, cor this is the life for me. It was all right when you weren't seasick, but when you were seasick it was a different matter.

From The Battle of the Atlantic, *Chris Howard Bailey; Royal Naval Museum/Alan Sutton Publishing, 1994.*

95

The 'News Chronicle'

The newspaper gives its readers 'the first full story' of the sinking of the German battleship, Bismarck.

From the Admiralty and the Air Ministry there came last night the first full account of the four days of Atlantic battle and pursuit which culminated at 11.1 A.M. yesterday [27 May 1941] in the sinking of the *Bismarck*, finest fighting ship in Hitler's fleet.

The 35,000 ton Nazi warship was hunted for more than 1,750 miles before she was sunk by torpedoes from the cruiser *Dorsetshire* almost 400 miles west of Brest.

The main body of the Home Fleet, under Admiral Sir J. C. Tovey on board the battleship *King George V*, a force from Gibraltar under Vice-Admiral Sir James Somerville… and the battleships *Rodney* and *Ramillies*, all answered the call: 'Get the *Bismarck*'.

These naval forces consisted of at least four battleships, two battle cruisers, two aircraft carriers, four cruisers and a number of destroyers led by the famous *Cossack*.

In addition, machines of the Canadian Air Force came out from Newfoundland to search, Coastal Command planes shadowed the quarry on the chase, while from the *Ark Royal* and the *Victorious* Fleet Air Arm planes swept the skies reporting every twist and turn of the *Bismarck* as she tried desperately to break through the gigantic net.

Private Cyril Doy, 6th Battalion, Royal Norfolk Regiment

Discovered very quickly that Pearl Harbor engendered in all Americans a determination to join in, fight and win the war.

In December 1941, I'd never heard of a place called Pearl Harbor. I was in a convoy on an American ship called the *Mount Vernon* heading for the Middle East. I remember the Americans on board were very upset about what had happened and I can remember one of them saying to us, 'Now we'll show you guys how to win a war.'

'Now we'll show you guys how to win a war.'

Imperial War Museum sound archive 23812, quoted in Forgotten Voices of the Second World War, *Max Arthur; Ebury Press, 2005.*

Naval engine room artificer Clifford Simkin

Clifford Simkin explains how his ship survived several trips through 'Bomb Alley' from Alexandria to Tobruk, guarding two ships supplying the besieged Libyan port.

… Off to Tobruk which was now [June 1941] isolated, in a state of siege…. We [on *Flamingo*] were the guardian angel over a couple of ships that were not worth a bomb, but when you have nothing better they are wonderful. We had another naval vessel with us, it may have been the *Grimsby*. We had not been to sea long before the Stuka raids started, and they hammered us all the way to Tobruk and back, the ships were carrying much-needed supplies, but they were slow which meant it took days to get there, suffering air attacks the entire time.

The waves of Stukas were in the region of thirty-five to forty-five and every now and again they sent in what we called a mixed bag, high-level bombers, Stukas and torpedo bombers or seaplanes. The high level would arrive first and while we were occupied the Stukas would come diving in and now there were two lots to worry about, then the torpedo-carrying aircraft crept in low on the horizon. The pom-pom four-barrel gun would concentrate on the torpedo-carrying aircraft, the spread of the exploding four shells covered a large area and the rate of fire was altered early in the war from 110 per barrel to 90 per barrel per minute.

Our skipper always called the main engines his main armament, because he used to manoeuvre the ship at speed to miss the sticks of bombs aimed at us.

The gun would be fired at the oncoming planes, then the firing would stop. The torpedo-carrying planes would turn to come in for the attack, then the gun would start firing again, the planes would drop their torpedoes in an attempt to save themselves. The torpedoes would be running towards us, we would turn to face the incoming tin fish and with luck they would pass along our side without hitting our hull. The four-inch and our smaller guns would be concentrating on the Stukas and high-level.

Our skipper always called the main engines his main armament, because he used to manoeuvre the ship at speed to miss the sticks of bombs aimed at us. Full ahead, full astern, then quick rudder movements to alter course.

Report document Simkin, C., 91/17/1 in the Documents Department of the Imperial War Museum.

Attack on Pearl Harbor

Thus began the Japanese attack on Pearl Harbor, which left the US Pacific Fleet in ruins and brought the United States into World War II.

Dawn was breaking over the US naval base of Pearl Harbor on the Hawaiian island of Oahu. From the bridge of the destroyer USS *Ward*, Lieutenant William W. Outerbridge caught sight of a small dark submarine conning tower in the water off his starboard bow. It was moving… along the channel leading to Pearl's main anchorage, in an area forbidden to American craft. Outerbridge ordered his main guns to open fire.

It was Sunday, December 7, 1941. At 6.45 am a 4 in (100mm) shell tore into the conning tower, and it sank from sight. Outerbridge reported the incident to his headquarters on shore…

[Soon] the *Ward* was once more a hive of activity. Its sonar had just detected another submarine. It released five depth charges, and a huge black bubble erupted astern as the sub was hit. Lieutenant Outerbridge reported this new incident to his headquarters. By now, its staff should have realised that something was badly wrong. But nearly an hour passed before duty officer Commander Vincent Murphy phoned Admiral Kimmel [Commander in Chief of the Pacific Fleet] with a garbled version of the morning's events. It was now 7.40 am.

From The World at Arms: The Reader's Digest Illustrated History of World War II; *Reader's Digest Association, 1989.*

Cyril Stephens

Cyril Stephens joined the Royal Navy in 1940 as a Hostilities Only seaman, serving on the 'Flower' class corvette, Orchis, *in the Atlantic for three years. He was demobilised as a petty officer in 1946, after serving for a year with the South East Asian Command in Ceylon.*

The corvette boys had great respect for the men in the Merchant Navy...

We had great respect for the Merchant seamen. I think they were underestimated, especially now by the British public…, because they talk about the Battle of Britain. Granted the pilots did a marvellous, marvellous job, but when you stop and think, how did they get the fuel across to fly those planes, it was the Merchant seamen. And if you've ever seen a tanker go up in flames, my golly! You hear this terrific roar and this one great sheet of flame and then there's nothing, just like that. And, honestly, I think they're the bravest men out, the Merchant Navy. The corvette boys had a great respect for the men in the Merchant Navy and likewise the Merchant Navy had for us, because they used to say, 'We don't know how you fellows live aboard them things, because sometimes we see a bit of funnel and then we don't see anything for a while, then we see a bit more funnel.'

From The Battle of the Atlantic, *Chris Howard Bailey; Royal Naval Museum/Alan Sutton Publishing, 1994.*

Military historian John Laffin

John Laffin finds a moment of relaxed heroism during the Battle of Midway, when the US Pacific Fleet's victory meant the end of Japanese naval supremacy in the Pacific.

[In the Pacific, American] casualties were great at sea…Many fighting men met their fate with a strangely flippant dignity. Three sailors were trapped five decks down in the sinking aircraft-carrier *Yorktown*, torpedoed at Midway 4th June 1942. An officer telephoned the men to ask if they knew the situation. 'Sure,' their spokesman said,' We know you can't get us out but we've got a helluva good acey-deucey game down here right now.'

> …Many fighting men met their fate with a strangely flippant dignity.

From Americans in Battle, *John Laffin; J.M. Dent and Sons Ltd., 1973.*

Sir Robert Atkinson, D.S.C.

A merchant navy man who became a midshipman in the Royal Naval Reserve. In 1940 he was appointed to the first of a bouquet of 'Flower' class corvettes – Rhododendron, Azalea, Snowdrop *and* Pink *– escorting the Atlantic convoys before taking command of the 'Castle' class corvette HMS* Tintagel Castle *in 1944.*

In the *Tintagel Castle* we got a contact [an acoustic torpedo echo] at half past five one night. We didn't sink that U-boat till six o'clock the next morning. Now that was doggedness and perseverance by the U-boat and by myself, in that he was very alert. He was a very experienced man. He kept turning. We dogged him. We didn't attack, we waited. We attacked and we stopped. We had limited ammunition on board, and it went on, and we probably followed him for an hour during the night. He probably thought he was away. We were trailing him. Finally we would attack him at change of watch when their crews were changing. We knew they would be changing at four o'clock in the morning, and finally, about half past six in the morning, at daylight, we went in… we had damaged him during the night … and we closed in and attacked him and got him. Now that's a long time to keep your concentration ….

From The Battle of the Atlantic, *Chris Howard Bailey; Royal Naval Museum/Alan Sutton Publishing Ltd, 1994.*

Roy F. 'Dick' Dykes, D.S.C., V.R.D.

Dykes was appointed a sub-lieutenant, RNVR, to the 'Flower' class corvette HMS Honeysuckle *in December 1940. His several years fighting the Battle of the Atlantic brought him numerous encounters with merchant seamen, few of them as unlikely as the one he describes here.*

We were bringing a convoy from Halifax.... It was attacked and the USS *Pink Star* was torpedoed, and we lowered the dinghy to pick up survivors, and we took a long time picking them up, because there were quite a number of survivors to rescue. Eventually the ship sank, and as it sank the fires went out, so we were completely in the dark, and by then also the small personal lights which each seaman carried on his shoulder would have gone out... We eventually came across a man who earlier had been singing hymns... We found him quite by accident. He was just floating with his life-jacket covered in oil and he was pretty well unconscious by the time we found him.

It had been about 25 minutes after the ship had sunk, and he was so heavy... we had to take him astern, take the rudder and tiller out of the dinghy and bring him over the stern.... He had two lifebelts on...[and] one leg that was very hard, as if it had been frozen.... We got him on board and he turned out to be all right. It also proved that this very hard leg was an artificial leg, so his two life-jackets were to keep him afloat. He was an elderly man, getting on for his late sixties, if not into the seventies. A retired American master mariner, he had come back into the American Merchant Navy to help this country – 'the old lady' as he called her – and inside his artificial leg were rolls upon rolls of American dollars,... which we dried out for him in the boiler room, and handed them back to him when we returned to Liverpool.

. . . and inside his artificial leg were rolls upon rolls of American dollars . . .

From The Battle of the Atlantic, *Chris Howard Bailey; Royal Naval Museum/Alan Sutton Publishing, 1994.*

Raymond Lund

Raymond Lund, 17 when he joined the Royal Navy in 1942, served on the destroyer, Scorpion, *guarding the Arctic convoys that supplied Russia.*

We were never dry. And if ever you went to change your clothes you had to do it very quickly as you never knew when 'action stations' would be called. We were often at action stations 22 hours a day.

There wasn't much sleep for anyone. When I did sleep it was fully clothed on a bench. I even slept standing up.

About 16 to 18 U-boats would form a line ahead of us. We used to charge through and disperse them. In the summer it was never dark, in the winter it was never light. We used to like a bit of rough sea. It may have been uncomfortable but it kept the U-boats away.

When it was cold, it was difficult to breathe… Never at any time could we touch metal. It would burn and stick to your fingers and it would mean a trip to the sick bay . . .

The most memorable day of the war for me was when we sank the *Scharnhorst*. It was Boxing Day 1943.… The *Duke of York* came up behind. There were two destroyers to her starboard and two to port. The *Scorpion* fired torpedoes at the *Scharnhorst* which slowed her up.…An Arctic fret obscured our view. We knew by a terrific explosion when she had gone. Our ship picked up over 30 survivors. We took them back to Scapa Flow.

From Handbook of World War II *by Karen Farrington; Abbeydale Press, 2006.*

Captain Harry Butcher, General Eisenhower's Naval Aide

Butcher stepped on board a battleship for the first time in the last days of the war in North Africa.

Yesterday [4 May 1943, in Algiers] I went with Ike to have lunch as guests of Admiral Willis, commanding officer of Force H, Royal Navy. It was on H.M.S. *Nelson*, sister ship of the *Rodney*, which was lying nearby.

Anticipating the formalities, Ike had asked a couple of days ago that I check to find out just what a general in his position should do when he goes aboard a battleship. Not ever having been on one myself, and me an alleged naval aide, I told him I would simply ask some of my Royal Navy friends to tell me just in what respect the British 'piping aboard' ceremony differs from the American. Ike asked what the hell would I say if asked to describe the American custom. He had me there. But I said I'd go to my friend Captain Jerry Wright, USN, and ask how the American service differed from the British. But I was vulnerable there, too, if cross-examined. Finally decided to make a full breast of my ignorance to Jerry. Before I could act, along came Flag Officer Dampier, Admiral Cunningham's aide, who gave me the lowdown. So I prepared Ike. All he had to do when he came up the gangplank was to salute straight ahead, just as he stepped over the rail. Then he would be conducted on a review of the guard that would be assembled to man the rail....

From Three Years with Eisenhower, *Captain Harry C. Butcher USNR; William Heinemann Ltd, 1946.*

Captain Harry Butcher, General Eisenhower's Naval Aide

Butcher tells how the Royal Navy took General Eisenhower to Sicily on D-Day + 1 in September 1943.

[General Eisenhower's] party for the Sicilian trip kept growing. It finally totalled eleven, some of whom were to stay.... We were driven to the Customs House, where we were met by an ancient barge of the Royal Navy. This resplendent craft had a brightly polished brass smokestack not unlike that of our old-time American fire wagon. But it was propelled by a petrol motor. In this we were taken across the Valletta harbour to one of its many 'deep creeks', which make it one of the finest natural harbours in the world, to the large destroyer H.M.S. *Petard*. She was lying alongside a tanker, taking on oil, and had just come away from Force H and en route to Malta had picked up a crew of a German plane which had been in a rubber boat ninety hours. After this crew had been revived they were taken on deck and shown the mighty fleet wallowing in the Mediterranean. They couldn't believe their eyes. Axis propaganda had repeatedly assured them the bulk of the Royal Navy long ago had been sunk.

Lieutenant Commander R. C. Egan, R.N., amiable skipper of the *Petard*, made us comfortable, gave us beer, and prepared for sailing at 2 a.m., which, at twenty-six knots, would put us offshore at Licata about sunrise.

From Three Years with Eisenhower, *Captain Harry C. Butcher USNR; William Heinemann Ltd, 1946.*

WAR ON THE
HOME FRONT

War on the Home Front

For one part of the United Kingdom, the Channel Islands, war with Germany meant occupation by the enemy, with increasingly severe hardship and deprivation for five long years. Saved from invasion and occupation, Britain still felt the effects of war in every aspect of life. Early responses to war, such as evacuating children, imposing a blackout, activating the ARP and other civil defence services, getting the call-up of men into the services underway, and bringing in food rationing caused a shake-up of everyone's lives.

Once the Blitz began in August 1940, the shake-up became profound. The nights for many people living in Britain's cities and with no safe shelters of their own were spent crowded into public shelters, some purpose-built, others, like the London Underground and many large office buildings with basements, converted to night-time shelter use. At first, Hitler confined his bombing of Britain to such places as airfields, ports and industrial sites. But when Britain responded by bombing strategic German cities including Cologne and Berlin (struck for the first time the day after London was bombed for the first time), Hitler, having given up all thought of preserving London intact so that he could walk up the Mall in triumph after a successful invasion, increased the bombing of London and extended it to Britain's great industrial cities and ports.

An RAF bombing attack on Lübeck, a non-industrial town, in March 1942, inspired Hitler to extend the Luftwaffe's bombings to such historic cities as Exeter, Bath, Norwich and York, chosen, it was said, from the German Baedecker tourist guide to Britain. Just a week after D-Day, 6th June 1944, when Britons first began to hope that the war might not last much longer, the first of Hitler's most fearsome weapons, the V1 and V2 flying bombs and rockets, began to rain down on England, triggering Operation Rivulet, a second wave of evacuations of children.

Even for those parts of the country – and there were many – that never heard an air-raid siren or experienced an air raid, it was not always easy to 'stay calm and keep going', as the famous wartime poster put it.

The lack of light that resulted from strict blackout rules, for instance, made going out after dark in towns and cities hazardous. And there were no welcoming lights outside cinemas, music halls and theatres, many of which gave up evening performances 'for the duration'. At least they were open: at the outbreak of war the government closed all cinemas and places of entertainment, fearing great loss of life if they were bombed. Quickly re-opened, cinemas, in particular, became hugely popular and the greatest morale booster and purveyor of propaganda of the war.

At home, where wartime light bulbs, hard to obtain anyway as the war went on, gave a rather dim light, it was often hard not to feel gloomy, despite the BBC's splendid morale-boosting output of radio comedy. Making homes as damage-proof as possible did not add to their comforts. For larger houses, there was often an understairs cupboard that could be converted to a shelter, but smaller houses had to make do with a sturdy kitchen table or a large and unwieldy Morrison shelter in the sitting room. If the house had a garden, then an Anderson shelter could always be constructed.

The question of food always loomed large on the home front. Feeding a nation of many millions in wartime, with food imports drastically cut or failing to arrive at all because of the enemy's constant attacks on merchant shipping in the Atlantic, meant a strictly imposed and increasingly draconian rationing system. It became a way of life for Britain's housewives and homemakers to stand in queues outside shops, clutching the family's ration coupon books, to buy what food was available and to cook it as carefully and as economically as possible, perhaps following one of the thousands of recipes issued by the Ministry of Food, or using tips heard on the morning's 'Kitchen Front' programme on the wireless.

Exhorted to 'Dig for Victory', people grew food, especially vegetables, everywhere they could: in their gardens, on the roofs of Anderson shelters, in parks, on bomb sites. Many people kept pigs, food for which might come from the pig swill bins set up in the street. The arrival of thousands of GIs in Britain in 1942 brought a welcome addition to the diets of children, who delighted in the generous way American servicemen handed out Hershey bars and other confectionery; their older sisters much preferred the nylon stockings the GIs also brought.

The war on the home front meant more than feeding and protecting people. Family life and society as a whole were turned upside down by the needs of wartime industry. Millions of men and women found themselves directed to unpleasant and difficult jobs in unfamiliar parts of the country to put up with poor working conditions and even poorer accommodation while doing essential war work in munitions and aircraft factories, in chemical plants, on docks, and, in the case of some 20,000 Bevin Boys, down coal mines.

The nearest thing to the Bevin Boys for Britain's women was the Women's Land Army, for which 90,000 women volunteered. The work was hard, the accommodation often dreadful, but many women revelled in the outdoor life. Thousands of women also worked in Civil Defence while carrying on with their usual day jobs. Women also did many jobs directly connected with the war, such as manning anti-aircraft ('ack ack') posts, looking after barrage balloons and flying new and repaired aircraft to the airfields where they were needed.

A Jersey woman remembers . . .

the first order to citizens on the day that the Bailiff of Jersey was forced to surrender to Germany, whose troops arrived in force in the Channel Islands on 2 July 1940. Some people, in order to make their disgust clear, hung out torn-up pillow cases, white knickers, vests and underpants with holes in them, even a baby's nappy.

The most tragic time of the day [1 July 1940] was when we were all informed that we all had to have a white flag of surrender flying from every house in the island by 7 a.m. on the Tuesday morning, the time when the Germans were to occupy the island. So we were all busy making and erecting this unhappy flag.

. . . we all had to have a white flag of surrender flying from every house in the island . . .

Quoted in Jersey: Occupation Remembered, *compiled by Sonia Hillsdon; revised edition, Seaflower Books, 2004.*

Virginia Woolf, writer

*Virginia Woolf describes in her diary the day she and her husband, Leonard, came under
fire during an aerial battle above her home in Sussex in September 1940.*

They came very close. We lay down under the tree. The sound was like someone sawing in the air just above us. We lay flat on our faces, hands behind head. Don't close your teeth, said L. They seemed to be sawing at something stationary. Bombs shook the windows of my lodge. Will it drop I asked? If so, we will be broken together. I thought, I think, of nothingness-flatness, my mood being flat. Some fear I suppose. Should we take Mabel to garage. Too risky to cross the garden, L. said. Then another came from Newhaven. Hum and saw and buzz all round us. A horse neighed in the marsh. Very sultry, Is it thunder? I said. No, guns, said L., from Ringmer, from Charleston way. Then slowly the sound lessened. Mabel in kitchen said the windows shook. Air raid still on: distant planes... Then the all clear 5 to 7. 144 down last night.

Too risky to cross the garden . . .

From A Writer's Diary, *edited by Leonard Woolf; Hogarth Press, 1953.*

Kenneth Morris

Teenager Kenneth Morris, working in a bank while waiting for his call-up, had first-hand experience of the Blitz at his home in Kew, west London. By January 1941 he and his Auntie Bess had both enrolled in the local fire-watching rota.

On 1 November [1940] I was working late at the bank. When I walked home the night raid had already started, illuminated by flares and searchlights. Planes and guns were noisy, and bursting shells dangerous. Although wearing my father's tin hat from the first world war, I had to take cover in a crowded shelter in Sandycombe Road. After continuing I was caught in Manor Road by a particularly heavy outburst of AA fire. Shrapnel hit the road and path on every side of me with small sparks, but I was unscathed....

On 15 November Tangier Road was struck by a 'Molotov bread basket'.

This contained a large number of widely scattered incendiaries. Air raid wardens hurried to put them out. Our neighbours extinguished one in our front garden by up-ending our hydrangea pot over it, thinking to have the laugh on us in the morning. But I was more preoccupied with the incendiary which fell through our roof into my bedroom, leaving its vane in the loft. It landed on top of a bookcase; fell behind, wedged on a ledge; and threatened to burn my books (and stamp album) and adjacent bed clothes. I raced upstairs with a bucket of sand to control the blaze and smoke.

Report document Morris, K. W., 87/44/1 in the Documents Department of the Imperial War Museum.

Ellen Harris, a Reuters Parliamentary press reporter

Ellen Harris was in London when the Blitz began in September 1940.

We got a bus, and we'd gone two or three hundred yards – as far as Islington Green – and the sirens went. Nobody knew what to do – this was the first ever. We'd had drill and training and what was impressed on everybody was the gas mask. And now, here was the first warning. Your mind immediately flew to the worst of everything. We were all turfed off the buses. Drivers, conductors, everybody, down into a shelter – we stopped right outside the Islington Green shelter. As we all went in – mothers carrying little babies with their gas mask on – the wardens were calling out 'Mind the live wires!' They hadn't finished the shelter. That was rather a shock.

> ## We were all turfed off the buses. Drivers, conductors, everybody, down into a shelter . . .

From Imperial War Museum sound archive 9820; in Forgotten Voices of the Second World War, *Max Arthur; Ebury Press, 2005.*

Evelyn Waugh, novelist

Evelyn Waugh depicts one aspect of London life during the Blitz in a letter to his wife, dated 11 November 1940.

...London looks much the same as it always did, the bomb craters at first sight might be the usual repairs & demolitions that are always going on. People's lives, on the other hand, are quite different. My first evening I dined at the Dorchester. Everyone was there from the Halifaxes to Bob Boothby and I had an agreeable evening meeting only friends. Phillis spends the day at Chapel Street, moves into the Dorchester in a room on the VIII floor at 6.30, moves down to the vestibule of Odham's suit & sleeps there from 11 until 7. Moves up to the VIII floor from 7 to 10. Others vary this routine by sleeping in the Turkish Bath instead of Odhams. There is absolutely no reason why the Dorchester should be any more secure than anywhere else but they feel happier near each other. A Fifth Column whispers that the hotel is not 'steel framed' and that the Turkish Bath has only two feet of rubble between it & the surface of Park Lane....

Next day I went to see Maimie who has moved from her big house to a cottage behind Brompton Oratory. She is living a life of serene detachment among acres of ruin.... When the party left we had a great luncheon of oysters and gruyère cheese, with two bottles of champagne. Then Vsevolode and I smoking cigars a yard long and Maimie smoking one of a good six inches, we went to a matinee. It is not at all London life as Hitler imagines it.

I hope to go North tomorrow, with little relish for the endless train journey.

There is no shortage of anything in London except lemons. Oysters are plentiful and are not 'fish'; neither are whitebait.

St James Piccadilly is bust up, also In & Out Club & a corner of Horse Guards. Otherwise no serious architectural losses that I saw.

...London looks much the same as it always did ... People's lives, on the other hand, are quite different.

From The Letters of Evelyn Waugh, *edited by Mark Amory; Weidenfeld & Nicolson, 1990.*

Vera Brittain, writer

Vera Brittain describes the atmosphere in the Majestic cinema, on the outskirts of Oxford, where up to a thousand refugees from the Blitz in the East End of London were given shelter for nearly two months before being found proper billets.

Covering the floor beneath the upturned velveteen seats of the cinema chairs, disorderly piles of mattresses, pillows, rugs and cushions indicate the 'pitches' staked out by each evacuated family. Many of the women, too dispirited to move, still lie wearily on the floor with their children beside them in the foetid air, though the hour is 11 a.m. and a warm sun is shining cheerfully over the city streets. Between the mattresses and cushions, the customary collection of soiled newspapers and ancient applecores is contributing noticeably to the odiferous atmosphere.

> Many of the women, too dispirited to move, still lie wearily on the floor with their children beside them . . .

From England's Hour, *Vera Brittain; Continuum Publishing, 1941.*

Sam

Eight-year-old Sam describes some of the odd side effects of the bombing of Coventry.

After that awful night [14 November 1940, when much of Coventry was reduced to rubble] we didn't bother with the shelter when the siren went; we tried to sleep in the cupboard under the stairs instead. Once, after another bad raid, we found the house opposite had been hit. Our front windows were gone, and there was broken glass everywhere. But what upset my mother terribly was that her curtains were in shreds.

Our front door had a leaded window. The lead had stretched in the heat, and the individual pieces of glass now looked like squares in a bar of chocolate.

> ...we tried to sleep in the cupboard under the stairs instead.

From Children of War, *Susan Goodman; John Murray, 2005.*

Chris O'Brien

Now living in Exeter, Chris O'Brien shared his memories of the Belfast Blitz with readers of The Times *in December 2008.*

The event that is etched in my memory was the Blitz in Belfast at Easter 1941. It was said that up to 1,000 people were killed. A large number were brought to St George's market, a large indoor fruit market, to be prepared for burial.

I was a 12-year-old altar boy at St Malachy's church and was picked to accompany the bishop for the burial ceremony. When I entered it was full of coffins but many were still being prepared for interment. Many were laid out on trestle tables and volunteer women were washing them down.... The bishop walked between the coffins with me on his tail holding the holy water that he sprinkled on the bodies as he passed....

Because of the religious divide two thirds peeled off at the city cemetery where Protestants were interred and one third continued to Milltown. I never did find out if they knew which was which. I often think that some diehard Nationalists lie in unconsecrated ground while an Orangeman is interred in a Fenian cemetery. It… brought home to me at an early age, that in the end, it didn't matter.

> The bishop walked between the coffins with me on his tail...

From The Times, *31 December 2008.*

Leslie Sinel

A Jersey man recorded in his diary on 8 June 1942 the latest restriction imposed by the German Occupying Forces on the Channel Islands.

What we had dreaded for a long time came to pass – all wireless sets belonging to the civilian population are to be handed in and retained in custody… infractions of this order are punishable by imprisonment of up to six weeks and a fine of 30,000 Reichsmarks (over £3,000).

'Bloody Germans!'

Unknown Jersey resident

A Jersey man who, like many islanders, kept his wireless set hidden from the Germans, describes a bit of quick thinking that kept it safe.

We kept our wireless and hid it up the chimney. The blacksmith made a couple of arms to keep it in place. All the neighbours used to come round to listen. One night we were all sat there in a circle listening to the news when there was a banging on the door. My brother went to see who it was. 'Who the hell is it?' I asked. 'Bloody Germans'. So we put a record on a very old rusty needle. The sound was terrible. 'Schöne Musik' said the German, as he saw everyone sitting round the gramophone.

Quoted in Jersey: Occupation Remembered, *compiled by Sonia Hillsdon; revised edition, Seaflower Books, 2004.*

Roger Brown

Now living in London, Roger Brown recalls in December 2008 in a letter to The Times *his early childhood in wartime Hull.*

I recall that night after night I was lifted out of bed as the siren sounded . . .

I was aged 7 in 1944. From 1940 onwards, when I lived with my parents on the outskirts of Hull, I recall that night after night I was lifted out of bed as the siren sounded and carried downstairs to the communal air raid shelter. In the shelter there was crowded warmth, cocoa, biscuits, bunks with stale blankets, quiet talk about whether the drone overhead was Jerry or one of ours, and the anti-aircraft battery thundering in the nearby park. One morning we emerged to find the eastern sky ablaze after the oil storage tanks in the port had been hit. For a young child, there was a feeling of excitement to be legitimately up and awake after midnight, and a participant in this very grown-up affair.

From The Times, *December 2008.*

Marjorie Meath

Marjorie Meath's husband was called up in 1940 so she decided to do her bit in Civil Defence, in her case fire fighting.

I applied to the AFS [Auxiliary Fire Service]. Asked if I wanted administrative or operational duties, I opted for the latter.

We were on 48/24 hour shifts (48 hours on/24 hours off).... First I learnt control duties, then switchboard. I was sent on an officer's training course but blew it because an officer said there were only 23 hours 59 minutes in a day, not 24 hours. I argued, saying that I could not accept that if a fire call came through at midnight, I had to write it in the control book as 23.59 or 00.01. I said it would be a lie. So every month,

when the divisional officer sent my name through for promotion it was that same officer who refused it. But I think I was happier in the ranks – they were such a wonderful crowd and there was such camaraderie between us.

> ... I think I was happier in the ranks – they were such a wonderful crowd ...

From Women at War 1939–1945, *Carol Harris; Sutton Publishing, 2000.*

Mary Whiteman

Recalls the effect of the arrival of American GIs in Britain in 1942.

But the American invasion had a great effect up on the town – a lot of drama, colour and romance. Social life certainly bucked up for girls, teenagers, young women and wives whose husbands were away – all sorts of things happened in Saffron Walden. I know two middle-aged women today who work in the baker's shop; they giggle when the Americans are spoken of. As teenagers, they used to try to get out in the evenings against their fathers' wishes to see them.... Some frowned upon it – there was a bit of anxiety about them. They were generous: they always had sweets to give to the

> ... they always had sweets to give to the children, and if a fair came to town ...

children, and if a fair came to the town – this did happen during the war – they'd treat all the children, but at the same time I imagine teenage daughters' mothers did worry and, of course, many did marry and go to America.

From Young Voices: British Children Remember the Second World War, *Lyn Smith; Viking, 2007.*

Edith Kent

Being just 4ft 11in tall enabled Edith Kent to crawl inside torpedo tubes during her wartime welding job, as she told The Times *when celebrating her 100th birthday with a tea dance in 2008.*

I got the job [as a welder in Devonport dockyard, Plymouth in 1941] because my brothers worked at the dockyard and they thought I would be good at it. I was the first woman to work as a welder there. It made me a bit uncomfortable that I was the first woman to earn the same as the men – and in some cases I was earning more than them. All the men I worked with were marvellous and they didn't seem to mind me earning the same [a skilled worker's wage, which was £6 6 shillings in 1943].

None of them ever dared say it, but I think they knew I was worth as much as them, if not more.

It made me a bit uncomfortable that I was the first woman to earn the same as the men . . .

From article in The Times, *27 November 2008.*

Food shortages

A Jersey resident remembers increasing food hardship on the island in the fourth year of the German occupation.

As we waited in the queue we used to ask each other 'I wonder what could be in that one' as people went up to collect their baking tins. One old man dropped all his roasted potatoes. So we all stopped and put them back for him.

We mixed the corn we made with water and salt and then took it round to the communal bake house. When it came out of the oven it was brown and hard and we had to cut it out of the tin. But if you are hungry enough you are grateful for anything. We called it 'hard bake'.

I used to cut all the vegetables up, put them in a big crock and take it to the bake house. You were given a number and it was also put on the crock. Then you would go and collect it when it was cooked.

One old man dropped all his roasted potatoes.

Quoted in Jersey: Occupation Remembered, *compiled by Sonia Hillsdon; revised edition, Seaflower Books, 2004.*

Marguerite Patten, food writer and broadcaster

Marguerite Patten joined the Ministry of Food as a Home Economist in 1942 and spent the war guiding women in how to get the best out of rationed foods.

The area in which I worked covered all East Anglia and I was responsible for a second Food Advice Centre in Ipswich. As much of this was a rural area where large amounts of fruit were grown, I had a number of sessions in charge of 'Fruit Preservation Centres' in schools or other large kitchens where groups of ladies would gather to make preserves from local grown fruit and specially supplied sugar. The recipes were sent by the Ministry of Food to ensure that the completed preserves could be stored and sold as part of the rations. The sessions were not entirely peaceful, for most ladies were experienced housewives, with their own very definite ideas on how jams should be made; some wanted to use their own recipes and addressed me firmly. 'Young woman, I was making jam before you were born' – quite right – but my job was to ensure that every completed pot of jam contained 60 % sugar and was carefully sealed to ensure it really would keep well under all conditions, so I had to stand firm.

. . . ladies would gather to make preserves . . .

From We'll Eat Again, *Marguerite Patten; Hamlyn, 1990.*

Hiding food

This man from a farming family in Trinity, Jersey, took a great risk in hiding food and raw ingredients from the Occupation forces.

They [the Germans] used to come round looking for wheat. We had some of our surplus buried under the floor, some hidden in cider casks. At the top of the casks were the apples, at the bottom the wheat. We were very nervous at the time of the inspections but nothing was ever found. One of those who came to inspect was a Dutchman. As he was almost as much on our side he was not very particular in his searching and he used to hand round cigarettes. We were just lucky.

> We were very nervous at the time of the inspections but nothing was ever found.

Quoted in Jersey: Occupation Remembered, *compiled by Sonia Hillsdon; revised edition, Seaflower Books, 2004.*

Geoff Baker

Geoff Baker had just left school and was waiting to go into the Royal Marines when he received his 'Bevin Boy' call-up papers just before Christmas 1943.

This is a load of rubbish, I thought. It used the word 'selected', as if I was privileged – I'll never forget that word. It was almost more than I could bear. I put the thing in a drawer, wildly thinking that with a bit of luck anything relating to me would be lost in the Christmas rush. Alas. For a lad whose school motto was *Quae sursum sunt quaerite* [Seek those things which are above] I seemed to be going in the wrong direction.

> It used the word 'selected', as if I was privileged – I'll never forget that word.

From Called Up Sent Down: The Bevin Boys' War, *Tom Hickman; The History Press, 2008.*

Bill Hitch

Bill Hitch was a market gardener when he was called up to work in the coalmines.

I had a good putter [hauling was called 'putting' in many coalmines] mate, another Bevin Boy called Bobbie Cave, who came from Liverpool – two putters to take out six men's coal. The first day there was talk of those six men would never get their work out with two Bevin Boys putting off them. Bobbie and me made our minds up that we would disprove this. Each hewer filled 12 tubs, so Bobby and me had to putt 36 tubs each. And we did, plus three full tubs that went to our name and were worth a couple of bob [shillings] apiece. We won the respect of all the men in the pit, but it was hard. People can have no idea.

We won the respect of all the men in the pit, but it was hard.

From Called Up Sent Down: The Bevin Boys' War, *Tom Hickman; The History Press, 2008.*

Edith Hollinshead

*Wife of Montague 'John' Hollinshead, an officer in corvettes doing escort duty in the
Atlantic, led in Liverpool a quiet, lonely life that many another World War II serviceman's
wife would have recognised.*

There was nothing else to do, anyway, just sit in the room.

… Time went very slowly and four years is a long time – five in my case because he didn't come back till, I think it was August '46. Still, I got the home ready. We bought a house and that was ready when he came back.

I don't think he had an official leave; he just came into port and that was it.

For refitting, or whatever they were doing, and then we used to see each other for three or four days. No, he just turned up. I was always there. There was nothing else to do, anyway, just sit in the room. I had a lovely view of the water, midnight sun; it was quite nice. But it was very lonely.

From The Battle of the Atlantic, *Chris Howard Bailey; Royal Naval Museum/Alan Sutton Publishing Ltd, 1994.*

Albert Beckers

Albert Beckers and his family were in their house in the centre of Cologne on one of the biggest nights of bombing in 1943, when 608 aircraft of Bomber Command reduced much of the great German city to blazing, oxygenless rubble.

The aircraft engines made the air vibrate. We were like rabbits in a warren. I was worried about the water pipes. What would happen if they burst and we were all drowned? The air shook with detonations. Stuck in the cellar we hadn't felt the hail of incendiaries but above us everything was ablaze. Now came the second wave, the explosives. You cannot imagine what it is like to cower in a hole when the air quakes, the eardrums burst from the blast, the light goes out, oxygen runs outs and dust and mortar crumble from the ceiling.

> The air shook with detonations. Stuck in the cellar we hadn't felt the hail of incendiaries but above us everything was ablaze.

Quoted in Bomber Boys, *Patrick Bishop; Harper Perennial, 2008; the quote is a translation from* Köln im Bombenkrieg, 1942–1945, *Hans-Willi Hermans; Wartburg, Gudensberg-Gleichen, 2004.*

Ellen Harris, a Reuters reporter in Parliament

Ellen Harris's pleasure at the news of D-Day in 1944 was quickly dispelled by the arrival of Germany's latest weapon, the V1 'flying bomb'.

In 1944 Parliament had decided to sit in Church House opposite Westminster School [the House of Commons was bombed and burnt out in May 1941]. I was walking from Dean's Yard to Westminster Station when a doodlebug came over. The doodlebugs would cut out then come backwards and drop. I was terrified but I didn't want to show it. Would I run? No fear! Nobody else was running – I wasn't going to run. If a single person had thrown himself down into the gutter, I'd have followed but no-one did. No-one.

> The doodlebugs would cut out then come backwards and drop.

Imperial War Museum sound archive 9820; from Forgotten Voices of the Second World War, *Max Arthur; Ebury Press, 2005.*

Fitzroy Maclean

Fitzroy Maclean, after months as commander of the British military mission to the Jugoslav Partisans, was invited to Chequers in July 1943 to brief the Prime Minister on the situation in the Balkans.

When I reached Chequers, I wondered if the Prime Minister would ever find time to talk to me about Jugoslavia. The Chief of the Imperial General Staff was there, and Air-Marshal Harris, of Bomber Command, and an American General, and an expert on landing-craft, and any number of other people, all of whom clearly had matters of the utmost importance to discuss with Mr. Churchill. Red leather dispatch boxes, full of telegrams and signals from every theatre of war, kept arriving by dispatch rider from London.

Then there were the films; long films, short films, comic films and serious films, sandwiched in at all hours of the day and night. The great men stood by, waiting their turn, hoping that it would not come in the early hours of

. . . all of whom clearly had matters of the utmost importance to discuss with Mr. Churchill.

Red leather dispatch boxes, full of telegrams and signals from every theatre of war, kept arriving by dispatch rider from London.

the morning, a time when the ordinary mortal does not feel at his brightest, especially if he has seen three or four films in succession, but when the Prime Minister, on the contrary, seemed filled with renewed vigour of mind and body.

Towards midnight, in the middle of a Mickey Mouse cartoon, a memorable interruption took place. A message was brought in to Mr. Churchill, who gave an exclamation of surprise. Then there was a scuffle and the film was stopped. As the squawking of Donald Duck and the baying of Pluto died away, the Prime Minister rose to his feet. 'I have just received some very important news. Signor Mussolini has resigned.' Then the film was switched on again.

From Eastern Approaches, *Fitzroy Maclean; Jonathan Cape, 1949.*

Cyril Stephens

When ashore on leave, Cyril Stephens showed the same quick thinking that he needed on board his corvette, HMS Orchis.

When we were based in Greenock and Gourock, we used to take the little train up to Glasgow, and the first port of call was the Glasgow Empire. I loved the theatres and all the shows then. We were lucky because one of our members' wives worked in the ticket office at the Glasgow Empire, and so she had a rough idea of when we would be home and so she used to hang on to a few tickets, just in case…. I remember once Maurice Wilikin's Daughters of Lovelace were appearing and one of the stewards came down during the interval and said they wanted two sailors to lead Britannia down the steps for the grand finale. And I said, 'Right, that's me.' So I went up with another one of our ship's company and we led Britannia down the steps, and so I can honestly say I appeared on the Glasgow Empire stage.

> … she used to hang on to a few tickets, just in case …

From The Battle of the Atlantic, *Chris Howard Bailey; Royal Naval Museum/ Alan Sutton Publishing Ltd, 1994.*

THE BEGINNING
OF THE END

The Beginning of the End

The invasion of Europe from Britain, which Winston Churchill had looked forward to in November 1942 as the beginning of the end of World War II, was first discussed at the Allied leaders' Casablanca conference of January 1943. Here, it was agreed that the invasion, code-named 'Operation Overlord', would not be launched before May 1944. The Anglo-Canadian Dieppe Raid in August 1942, a hugely costly disaster, had at least taught several valuable lessons: a well-defended coast or port in enemy hands could not be attacked and seized head on; the place of invasion would have to be very carefully chosen; there would have to be much pre-invasion 'softening-up' of the territory; and

there would have to be very careful planning for months in advance. Secrecy would also be essential.

In the months leading up to D-Day, southern England and its Channel coast, from Torquay in the west to Shoreham in the east, became a vast military camp, as much as possible of its manpower and equipment hidden from enemy air reconnaissance and intelligence in woods and under hedges, in barns and in camouflaged places, lined up in the streets of towns and villages. There was also a rather less well hidden invasion site, complete with fake oil storage depot (visited with some publicity by the King and Queen), on the coast near Dover, within sight of Calais. This was designed to make the enemy believe that if an invasion came from Britain it would be directed over the shortest Channel crossing, the Straits of Dover.

The amphibious and airborne Allied assault on Normandy that began in considerably less than ideal weather at 12.16 a.m. British time on D-Day 6 June 1944 was an invasion of a size and complexity never before seen in the world. On that first day, more than 150,000 men and thousands of military vehicles were landed on the coast of Normandy, often under heavy enemy fire.

The troop-laden warships of Operation Neptune, the seaborne part of Operation Overlord, sailed from Torquay, Weymouth, Portsmouth and Shoreham to rendezvous in a mid-Channel reception area. From here, the troops transferred to landing craft – described by the writer Ernest Hemingway as 'coffin-shaped'– for the landing on the Normandy beaches. As dawn broke, the Allied warships massed offshore began a series of massive bombardments of the German defences. Overhead, 9,000 aircraft, from Spitfires to Flying Fortresses, carried out wave after wave of aerial attacks.

Until the night before they sailed, none of the land forces' unit commanders knew that the landing sites and objectives they had been studying in great detail for weeks were in Normandy. The landings took place on five separate beaches, code-named Sword, Juno, Gold, Omaha and Utah, stretching from the Caen Canal westwards to just beyond the town of Ste-Mère-Eglise. French, British and Canadians landed on Gold, Juno and Sword and Americans on Omaha and Utah. The greatest number of casualties occurred on Omaha Beach, where 3,000 Americans were mowed down by the German defenders on the cliff-tops above. Even here, a good-sized beach head had been established by the time night fell.

The Allied planners had assumed that, once firmly settled on shore, their forces would be able to make steady progress inland and move inexorably through France and Western Europe towards Germany. But the enemy, sent reeling by the initial invasion, held grimly on to the city of Caen, brought up its powerful panzer reserves and made ready to resist to their last man. Caen was not finally taken until 9 July, having endured attack and bombardment that left the town in ruins.

Only after seven weeks of heavy fighting in the towns, villages and narrow lanes between high-banked hedges that marked the Normandy countryside, did the Germans at last retreat from the Falaise pocket into which they had been driven, abandoning thousands of tons of equipment as they went. On 25 July, Lieutenant General Omar Bradley's First US Army began its move out of Normandy, ponderously at first and then much more rapidly. On 25 August, Paris was liberated.

Even now, nearly two months after the Normandy Landings, the Allies were still only at the beginning of the end in Europe. Ahead lay an autumn of heavy fighting for the Allied armies advancing across Europe along a 1000-mile (1600km) front from the North Sea Coast of the Low Countries in the north to the eastern end of the Swiss frontier in the south. The Germans, with their backs to the River Rhine, the last natural obstacle on the way to the heart of Germany, made the Allies fight for every mile of the way – none more so than the 83,000 American soldiers in the Ardennes section of the front.

It was not until March 1945 that the Rhine was crossed at last. It was by a stroke of luck that the bridge at Remagen was found intact, which allowed units of the US Army to get over. The end of the Third Reich was in sight.

General Fritz Bayerlein

General Bayerlein, the commander of the Panzer Lehr Division in Normandy, still felt bitter many years later when he thought about the stubborn inflexibility of the German High Command in June 1944.

At 2 o'clock in the morning of 6th June I was alerted that the invasion fleet was coming across the Channel. I was told to begin moving north that afternoon at 5 o'clock. Well, this was too early. Air attacks had been severe in the daylight and everyone knew that everything that could fly would support the invasion. My request for a delay until twilight was refused. So we moved as ordered and immediately came under Allied air attack. I lost twenty or thirty vehicles by nightfall. At daylight next morning, the commander of the 7th Army gave me a direct order to proceed and there was nothing else I could do so the vehicles moved off as ordered.

By the end of the day I had lost forty trucks and ninety others. Five of my tanks were knocked out and eighty-four half-tracks, prime movers and self-propelled guns. These were serious losses for a division not yet in action.

Five of my tanks were knocked out . . .

From The Normandy Battles, *Bob Carruthers and Simon Trew; Cassell & Co., 2000.*

Veteran war photographer Robert Capa

Robert Capa chose to go ashore on D-Day with the Americans assigned to Omaha beach because he thought it would be interesting. It nearly cost him his life.

The water was cold, and the beach still more than a hundred yards away. The bullets tore holes in the water around me, and I made for the nearest steep obstacle. A soldier got there at the same time, and for a few minutes we shared its cover. He took the waterproofing off his rifle and began to shoot without much aiming. The sound of his rifle gave him enough courage to move forward, and he left the obstacle to me. It was a foot larger now, and I felt safe enough to take pictures of the other guys hiding just like I was.

I finished my pictures and the sea was cold in my trousers. Reluctantly, I tried to move away from my steel pole, but the bullets chased me back every time. Fifty yards ahead of me, one of our half-burnt amphibious tanks stuck out of the water and offered me my next cover. I sized up the situation. There was little future for the elegant raincoat heavy on my arm. I dropped it and made for the tank. Between floating bodies I reached it, paused for a few more pictures, and gathered my guts for the last jump to the beach.

Now the Germans played all their instruments, and I could not find any hole between the shells and bullets that blocked the last twenty-five yards to the beach. I just stayed behind my tank . . .

From Slightly Out of Focus, *Robert Capa; Henry Holt, New York, 1947.*

Cyril Timms

Cyril Timms recalls his part, played out on one of the ships in the huge Allied fleet, in Operation Overlord, which began with the D-Day landings in Normandy.

We came under attack several times . . .

When we were bombarding Normandy, we were anchored at Le Havre. We were bombarding twenty miles inland, a place called Caen. Incredible. We were being controlled, gunnery wise, by a spotter plane, twenty miles away. I don't know what the Germans thought, I'm sure. It certainly kept them on their feet when we put a few big shells amongst them.

The number of ships in the Channel that day was absolutely phenomenal. Thousands and thousands. The sea was black with ships. I'm surprised there weren't more collisions, and the sky was black with aircraft as well. I'm surprised they didn't have more accidents in the air than on the sea.

All the Allied ships were marked, as were the aircraft, with three stripes down each wing at that particular time. RAF, the ships and aircraft, were easily identified by these markings....

We came under attack several times but we weren't actually hit on the D-Day, but coming back to refuel and reload with armaments we hit a mine off the Isle of Wight and that threw the ship into confusion; a gaping great hole in the side.

From The Normandy Battles, *Bob Carruthers and Simon Trew; Cassell & Co., 2000.*

Sergeant Major Hans Erich Braun of 2nd Panzer Division

The sergeant major experienced the horrors of the Falaise pocket into which the Allies forced the last of the German divisions active in Normandy on D-Day. The capture of this pocket ended the battle of Normandy and began the real battle for Europe.

[It was a case of] forward through hell, but also towards the enemy, past the dead and the wounded. We had been tempered, like the steel plating of our tanks... We were alive, but inside dead, numbed by watching the horrible scenes which rolled past on both sides... anyone dying on top of those rolling steel coffins was just pitched overboard so that a living man could take his place.

The never-ending detonations – soldiers waving to us, begging for help – the dead, their faces screwed up in agony – huddled everywhere in trenches and shelters, the officers and men who had lost their nerve – burning vehicles from which piercing screams could be heard... [men]driven crazy, crying, shouting, swearing, laughing hysterically – and the horses, some still harnessed to the shafts – screaming terribly, trying to escape the slaughter on the stumps of their hind legs. But also there were civilians...still clinging to [their belongings] even in death....

The never-ending detonations . . .

From The World at Arms: The Reader's Digest Illustrated History of World War II; *Reader's Digest Association, 1989.*

US artilleryman Alfred Allred

Alfred Allred entered Paris with the Allies on 25 August 1944, the US 12th Infantry Regiment meeting up with a French armoured column. There were still Germans and collaborators sniping from the Bois de Boulogne when General de Gaulle, magnificently unconcerned, paraded down the Champs Elysées the next day.

We got into Paris, went by the Eiffel Tower and the Arc de Triomphe… The French girls, beautiful girls, some of them – those girls were climbing all over us, and giving us flowers.

Some of those girls had the most beautiful teeth. They must have been getting good food somewhere. Some of them were even wearing make-up.

> Some of the girls had the most beautiful teeth. They must have been getting food from somewhere.

From Voices from D-Day, *Jonathan Bastable; David & Charles, 2004.*

Mrs Iris Bullen

Pages from the wartime diary of Jersey mother Mrs Iris Bullen, whose husband served in the British Army during the war.

November 1944

We have had a Red Letter day, the importance of which cannot be realised, but only by those who suffer in these Islands and have undergone what we have in the last 4 and a half years, especially since the Invasion [of Europe on D-Day] last June when our islands have had to rely mostly on what they can produce, which does not cover a great number of essential things for our welfare. So today has brought joy to our hearts to hear of a Red Cross relief boat having been promised us with medical supplies, soap and food parcels. We do nothing but plan for that great day when our share will be in our possession.

On December 7th we heard the good news that our boat was due to leave Lisbon today en route for Guernsey and then to Jersey.

> So today has brought joy to our hearts to hear of a Red Cross relief boat . . .

Quoted in Jersey: Occupation Remembered, *compiled by Sonia Hillsdon; revised edition, Seaflower Books, 2004.*

Sergeant Kenneth Morris

Sergeant Kenneth Morris watched the Allied airborne assault across the Rhine from the 4th Armoured Brigade's main HQ, near Sonsbeck, 60 miles (100km) from the front line town of Goch.

Early on 24 March [1945] on a broad front the Allies' assault across the Rhine began. At 9.45 a.m., alerted by a steady roar, we watched wave after wave of airborne troops pass over. Because of the heat haze the parachutists' descent was out of sight, but the Dakota aircraft soon returned. Alternating with the troop carriers, 45 at a time, came long strings of gliders, two being towed behind each transport. These airborne operations lasted three hours. Four planes crashed in flames. Most of the crews parachuted to safety, but one unfortunate plunged like a stone when his chute failed to open. A stick of stores with red parachutes dropped in a nearby wood. In the afternoon, flights of four-engined Liberators came over very low to drop stores to the airborne troops, and suffered casualties.

> . . . but one unfortunate plunged like a stone . . .

Report document Morris, K. W., 87/44/1 in the Documents Department of the Imperial War Museum.

VICTORY

Victory

When Churchill, Roosevelt and Stalin met at the Yalta Conference in February 1945, the two Western leaders, given the strength of the Soviet Union's blitzkrieg charge through eastern Europe, were in no position to deny Stalin's demand that Poland should become a Soviet satellite. Thus, the war that Britain had gone into to defend Poland's territorial integrity ended with Poland losing its independence.

Although it was clear in February 1945 that the war would be over, in Europe at least, within months, if not weeks, Germany fought to the bitter end within Germany's boundaries and almost to the end, and sometimes after the formal surrender documents had been signed, in many other places. However bitterly the Germans fought in their last weeks, the end result was never in doubt once the Soviet armies had taken over eastern Germany. When the Americans, advancing from the west, met Soviet troops for the first time on 25 April, their meeting place was Torgau on the Elbe river. With so much of Germany at their backs, there was never any chance that the Soviet Union would allow the armies of the West any further east. Nazi Germany was split across its centre and it would be nearly fifty years before the two parts were reunited.

By this time, the full horrors of the Nazi regime in Germany had come to light with the liberation of concentration camps including Belsen and Buchenwald, which horrified and sickened Allied forces on 13 April. By this time, too, thousands of prisoners-of-war had had the joy of finding Allied, rather than German, troops at the gates of their camps.

Outside Germany, the war in Europe came to an end piecemeal. The Channel Islands, where conditions had been the harshest of the war after D-Day, got their first Red Cross shipment at New Year, 1945 but were not finally liberated until the day after VE Day. In Britain, the last two V2 rockets fired in the war landed on 27 March, one of them hitting a block of flats in east London and killing 134 people.

In Italy, where there had been a six-month stalemate since the autumn of 1944, the Allies launched a major offensive in early April; on 29 April the German commanders in Italy signed a surrender document at the Allied headquarters in Caserta, near Naples, which provided for the unconditional surrender of all German troops in Italy on 2 May. The war in Italy, which many of the men who fought in it felt had been forgotten after D-Day, had, in fact, been important because of the number of German troops who had been tied down in Italy when they were desperately needed back home. The Italian campaign was also notable for the wonderfully international make-up of the Allied forces. As well as British and American servicemen, the troops fighting the war in Italy included Australians, Canadians, New Zealanders, South Africans, Poles and Indians as well as Italian partisans and even a corps from Brazil.

One of Adolf Hitler's last acts, before killing himself in his Berlin bunker on 30 April, was to appoint Admiral Karl Dönitz head of state in his place. Thus, it was as Dönitz's representatives that three German officers presented themselves outside the three battered caravans that made up Field Marshall Montgomery's headquarters at Luneburg Heath, near Hamburg, on 3 May to surrender the German armies in Holland, Denmark and north-west Germany. The surrender document was signed the next day.

From Luneburg Heath, Donitz's representatives went to the headquarters in Rheims, France of the Supreme Allied Commander to discuss a complete surrender of German forces. Eisenhower refused to see them until an unconditional surrender on all fronts was signed – which it was on 7 May, taking effect from 1 minute past midnight, German time, on 9 May 1945. Prime Minister Winston Churchill and the new American President, Truman, had already decided

between them that they and their allies would celebrate VE (Victory in Europe) Day on 8 May.

The last months of the war against Japan were fought as savagely as all the months and years since December 1941, with the Japanese contesting every inch of the territory they had taken since Pearl Harbor. Inexorably – and, indeed, inevitably once the B-29 Superfortress precision bomber had been perfected in the USA and joined the USAAF in the Pacific – the Allies got closer and closer to Japan itself. Incendiary bombing of mainland Japan became increasingly effective in the early weeks of 1945. On 25 February 1945 came the first fire raid to hit Tokyo.

Although crippled in its efforts to wage war and in its ability to carry on everyday life in its towns and cities, Japan – or, rather, its military leaders – showed no sign of wishing to surrender. In August, the Allies brought out their biggest weapon, the atomic bomb. Shortly after 8 a.m. on Monday, 6 August 1945, a four-tonne atomic bomb, mildly named 'Little Boy', was dropped on the Japanese city of Hiroshima from a B-29 Superfortress, named 'Enola Gay' after its pilot's mother. This bomb was followed by a second, called 'Fat Man', on the city of Nagasaki on 9 August.

Three months after VE Day, World War II finally came to an end with the unconditional surrender of Japan on 14 August, with the world celebrating VJ Day on 15 August. The surrender documents were signed on board the USS *Missouri* on 2 September.

Lieutenant Commander Barry Barringer

Describes the last days of 835 Naval Air Squadron of the Fleet Air Arm, which spent most of the war, flying mainly from the aircraft-carrier Nairana, *defending Atlantic and Russian convoys from German U-boat and air attack.*

On our return from Norway, on 28 March, 1945, we received a signal that the Squadron was to be disbanded.

Although this was something that many of us had been half-expecting, it was nonetheless a shock to have it spelt out in black and white. We weren't sure whether to laugh or cry; laugh because we had come to the end of the road and were still alive, or cry because the friendships we had made and the camaraderie we had enjoyed were about to become things of the past.

There were some last rites: a last party in the wardroom, with Surtees [Capt. Villiers Surtees, captain of the carrier *Nairana*], all bonhomie, singing 'Fly off, fly off, for Christ's sake, the Captain wants a gong!'; a last beat up of the Fleet at anchor in Scapa Flow, with the most pukkah warships singled out for our most outrageous low flying and acrobatics; and finally our Swordfish and Wildcats flown for the last time to Evanton or Abbot to be 'mothballed'. It was like saying goodbye to old friends. We disbanded on 1 April.

We weren't sure whether to laugh or cry ...

From Alone on a Wide, Wide Sea, *E. E. Barringer; Leo Cooper, 1995.*

Lieutenant Colonel Trumbull Warren

Field Marshal Montgomery's Canadian personal assistant recalls the arrival of President of the Reich Dönitz's representatives at Montgomery's headquarters – three battered caravans on Luneburg Heath, near Hamburg, on 3 May 1945. The formal surrender document was signed – in a tent – the next day.

[Dönitz sent Admiral Hans von Friedeburg, Commander in Chief of the Navy, and three other officers to Montgomery's headquarters on 3 May, where] they stood to attention under the Union Jack....They faced the three caravans with the doors all closed. How long they stood there I do not know but it seemed like ages – it was probably four or five minutes, and they never moved. Quietly the door of the centre caravan opened and there stood a rather short Anglo-Irishman, wearing khaki trousers and battledress [and his familiar black beret with two badges – the field marshal's crossed batons and the Royal Tank Regiment badge].

... they stood to attention under the Union Jack ...

From The World at Arms: The Reader's Digest Illustrated History of World War II; *Reader's Digest Association, 1989.*

Troop commander Jack Swaab

Jack Swaab, who had taken part in the Rhine Crossing in March 1945, was with the 51st Highland Division in Germany when they were finally able to celebrate the end of the war in Europe in typical army style.

4 May. Over the wireless a quarter of an hour ago came the voice of the announcer – 'All German forces in NW Germany, Holland, Denmark and Heligoland have surrendered to Marshal Montgomery's 21st Army Gp.' All over the village [Bremervoerde, Germany], Brens are firing into the air, flares are going up and even the Germans are out in the street as the word spreads rapidly around which really marks the end of the journey begun when Mr. Churchill told the Germans in those long dark days – 'We shall never surrender!'. It seems strange to think that I may (repeat MAY) never have to risk my life in battle again.

6 May. *Afternoon, Hertogenbosch:* Started at 0830 yesterday and arrived here at 2045 with two half hour halts for repairs. Distance exactly 310 miles. The evening before, Debroy had come in and we'd all had a few drinks and then I went round the troop where everybody was loosing off Bren guns, Stens, pistols and Very lights; as far as the eye could see the sky was green and red, orange, mauve and white and the cheers and rattle of small arms made the night full of noise. I was reminded of Benghazi in 1942.

From Field of Fire, *Jack Swaab; Sutton Publishing, 2005.*

Celia Johnson, actress

While Celia Johnson was filming Brief Encounter *at Denham Studios in Buckinghamshire, she wrote this letter to her husband, Peter Fleming, on VE Day.*

My darling, we have really won the war and I can't believe it… To start with we all got into a state of rising excitement culminating on Monday when rumours were rife and all expected the news of victory from moment to moment. At the studio excitement became intense at lunchtime by the report that all Technicolor cameras had gone up to the Palace and bets were laid and work haphazard on account of having to rush out to listen to the radio between every shot. A sign of the tremendous upheaval was stressed by the unprecedented buying of a bottle of rather nasty white wine by Tony Havelock-Allan at lunch-time on our table.

To start with we all got into a state of rising excitement culminating on Monday . . .

From an article in The Times, *18 December 2008, written by Celia Johnson's daughter, Kate Grimond.*

Ellen Harris, a Reuters Parliament reporter

Ellen Harris was in the House of Commons, and in the streets with hundreds of thousands of Londoners, on VE Day.

I shall never forget it. I couldn't move – I couldn't do anything, whatever had happened. Although we'd known this was coming, the House of Commons itself just went into one great roar of cheers, papers went up in the air, I just sat and the tears were rolling down – it was a relief after all this long time. And this kept up, the roaring and cheering and shouting for some time. And then the Speaker dissolved the House....

[My husband and I] went to Whitehall, Charing Cross. We got through gradually. I was underneath the Ministry of Health Balcony –

thousands and thousands of people packed tight. They shouted and shouted for Churchill. Nobody was quite certain where he was but he came out on that balcony and he threw his arms out. He said, 'God bless you all,' and said a few words. He praised them for their fortitude – they had won the war, he said. He thanked them all – it was short and sweet but lovely for the Londoners. And he finished up once more, 'God bless you all!' The cheers – it was a wonder the clouds didn't come down. It was a really most momentous occasion.

I shall never forget it.

From Imperial War Museum sound archive 9820; in Forgotten Voices of the Second World War, *Max Arthur; Ebury Press, 2005.*